PᴇᴀᴄᴇQ

Increasing the Capacity For Peace Within
and Peace Beyond

Raise Your PQ!

By Jennifer Freed PhD

ISBN 978-0-692-62825-6
COPYRIGHT 2016 Jennifer Freed
MERMAIDS PRESS

Cover Art by Kyle Jean Brace

Table of Contents

PeaceQ

Whereas IQ measures certain aspects of brain intelligence and EQ measures certain aspects of emotional intelligence, PeaceQ (PQ) measures our ability to be peaceful within ourselves, peaceful with others, and to facilitate peace in our communities.

Preface/
About the Author

I have been working on this book my whole life. I have spent the last 30 years as a family therapist, a graduate school educator, a published author, a nonprofit executive director, and have been working in the field of social and emotional intelligence the entire time. I have been dedicated to uplifting myself, my beloveds, and my community.

They say you teach what you need to learn, and I would say you also seek to learn what you need to teach others. Temperamentally, I possess a short fuse and a large rebellious streak. I have been using the principles you will read in this book to "tame the tiger" and put my rebelliousness to good work.

I grew up in a home and cultural period marked by trauma and grief. My childhood contained constant anger and yelling. My oldest brother bullied me, and I bullied younger neighbors. I was five when John F. Kennedy was assassinated; I wept all day long that day. The Watts riots made a deep impression on me.

I was devastated by the murders of Martin Luther King, Jr. and Bobby Kennedy. I still cry when I hear the song "Abraham, Martin, and John" by Dion (1969):

Has anybody here seen my old friend Abraham?
Can you tell me where he's gone?
He freed a lot of people,
But it seems the good die young;
But I just looked around and he's gone.

Has anybody here seen my old friend John?
Can you tell me where he's gone?
He freed a lot of people,
But it seems the good die young;
But I just looked around and he's gone.

Has anybody here seen my old friend Martin?
Can you tell me where he's gone?
He freed a lot of people,
But it seems the good die young;
But I just looked around and he's gone.

Didn't you love the things that they stood for?
Didn't they try to find some good for you and me?
And we'll be free.
Someday soon, it's gonna be one day.

Has anybody here seen my old friend Bobby?
Can you tell me where he's gone?
I thought I saw him walkin' Up over the hill,
With Abraham, Martin, and John.

I wore armbands and protested against the Vietnam War at age 11. The Charles Manson murders happened terrifyingly close to where I grew up. As a teenager, I was sexually assaulted and knew too many young women who had been raped. When my high school began a "busing" program as I neared graduation, a color-coded pecking order soon emerged in our classrooms, giving me a firsthand perspective on the scourge of prejudice. In college, I joined a peace activist group and walked away completely disillusioned. The leaders were often lying to one another, exploiting young women, and sleeping with each other's partners on the sly. How could people working for peace treat the people closest to them so atrociously?

Even as I had been working diligently in my twenties on social and emotional learning programs to help young people, violence continued to deeply impact my life. In my thirties, I experienced the horror of violent suicide when my nephew shot himself on Mother's Day. The stress and cruelty of that event tore through me like a knife and brought my mother to her knees.

Then came 9/11, and the carnage of the Iraq war–two of my family friends suffered deeply from trauma sustained in active duty. More recently, mentally tortured Elliot Rodgers murdered six students in a town near my home, leaving that community in emotional shreds.

Unfortunately, my history with violence is not unique. We all have scarring stories and links to small and large-scale violent atrocities.

Our world has achieved unimaginable technological progress; yet we have far to go to attain peaceful and nonjudging hearts and safe homes and cities. No matter how many locks are on the walled and gated communities we create, not one of us lives in a peaceful world until we all do. My friend Hannah Baptiste reminds us that until we address systems and structures which perpetuate desperate conditions such as homelessness, poverty, lack of affordable medical services and education for all, we cannot fully address PEACEQ.

The impact of one youth being beaten to death, or one young person losing their life from hate and bigotry, or another person joining a gang because that is where they feel cared for, is a scar on our collective conscience. Many of us are addressing these issues daily. We do better if we can all come together to resolve these issues.

I was lucky. On my journey through the trauma of violence, I have always found mentors who could help heal me and teach me ways to help others. At 19, I found my calling as a social and emotional educator for teenagers and families. This passion to empower teens has grown even more ardent as I age; in 1999, it influenced my partner, Rendy Freedman, and me to create the nonprofit organization, AHA! (Attitude. Harmony. Achievement.). AHA! was created in response to the Columbine Massacre, with the idea that no youth should ever feel that desperate, that alone, that self-destructive, or that filled with hate. We started AHA! with the simple idea (borne out later by research—see the meta- analysis by Thomas Pettigrew and Linda Tropp on prejudice) that if young people truly got to know each other, played with each other, and developed empathy and connection, they would be far less likely to harm each other and would, in fact, be motivated to stand together as allies.

AHA! began as a small summer program with 20 youth and 14 creative arts and social and emotional learning facilitators. We now refer to that beginning as the "summer of love" because all the adults and teens reported that it was the best summer experience of their lives. Since then, with the help of dozens of exceptionally gifted and trained staff, AHA! has served thousands of teens and has started a grass roots movement of PeaceQ. Now, in my fifties, I see how converging points of personal and cultural pain and the extraordinary teachers and mentors I have met have inspired the idea of PeaceQ and this book. Without peace within each of us and peace between us, we all live an impoverished life. This book is my passionate nudge for a leap in our evolution of consciousness.

My hope is that humanity will become as fervently invested in PeaceQ—the ability to be peaceful within, to be peaceful with others, and to facilitate peace in our communities—as it has been in political campaigns or conspicuous consumption. I believe we can make this shift and make the most important evolution of the human race: the conscious taming of the limbic system in service of our higher ideals of companionship and community.

Peace is not a relationship of nations. It is a condition of mind brought about by serenity of soul. Peace is not merely the absence of war. It is also a state of mind. Lasting peace can come only to peaceful people.

– Jawaharial Nehru

We can become more than our basest instincts if we work persistently on developing pathways of peace in our brains and in our hearts. This handbook is designed to help you cultivate those pathways by expanding awareness and action in three areas:

1. Learning how to be more peaceful inside ourselves

2. Learning how to create satisfying and harmonious relationships with others

3. Learning how to actively cultivate loving and peaceful connections in our communities

The book is divided into three sections, each of which covers one of these three pieces of the peace puzzle.

This book is purposefully not laden with research studies, verified evidence, and data, although you can find all of this and more in the bibliography. It is friendly, conversational, and easy to share with others: something you can pick up any time to refresh your mind and your skills. PeaceQ is, essentially, a common-sense practice, applied with patience and persistence to yield ever-growing skill. Its treatment here is true to all the greatest teachings from every age, which point us in the same direction of love, happiness, and peace.

It is now our turn, each of us, to embody these wise and ancient teachings in mind, body, spirit through daily practice.

This book is dedicated to all the dreamers. I know I am not the only one.

Introduction:
Your Aim Is True

In our society, we seem to address the issue of peace after something goes terribly wrong or violence erupts. As a result, we come at the problem reactively instead of proactively, often without calm thinking and planning.

> *Peace cannot be kept by force; it can only be achieved by understanding.*
>
> – Albert Einstein

Consider these AGAINST statements:

"We need anti-bullying programs."

"We need to fight against prejudice."

"We have to win the war on drugs."

These statements force the brain to process negative meanings before it can move into the desired state.

AGAINST statements feel more urgent and dramatic—and, therefore, more compelling—than FOR statements, such as:

"We need programs to help everyone feel safe and fully accepted."

"We need to celebrate diversity and bring people from all walks of life together for shared understanding."

"We want to have a country where all people are healthy and can live healthy, happy lives."

Negative, AGAINST statements activate the warrior archetype in us; they can feel motivating. But they put us AGAINST others. They create a sense of defensiveness and righteousness. Oppositional strategies create separation and conflict even as they purport to vanquish social ills.

> *Resentment is like drinking poison and then*
> *hoping it will kill your enemies.*
>
> – Nelson Mandela

"Being-against" elicits hatred, anger, and fear, emotions that hijack the brain to a state of alertness. Sometimes, if the emotion is intense, it can send us into fight, flight, freeze, or faint. This emotionally volatile, or "triggered" state, is not compatible with patient, sustainable efforts to create change. With so much of media aimed at activating hate, fear, and anger against those with whom we disagree or to the things which we are opposed, we have become a nation of highly anxious and depressed people. We are so accustomed to being either in fight-or-flee mode, or collapsed in exhaustion or overwhelm, that we don't even realize we're stuck there.

In the wake of the Charleston church shooting in 2015, a new wave of "don't bully!" and "don't hate!" led white people to show up at black churches and to stand with black people in protests. While this is a laudable impulse—to respond to hatred with a resounding "No more!"—I don't want to wait for tragedy to do the right thing.

Campaigns to end things work only temporarily, or don't work at all.

Initiatives designed to eradicate what we don't want have been tried and thoroughly tested. We've seen the War on Drugs, the War on Poverty, the War on Cancer, and a thousand well-intentioned anti-bullying initiatives. In spite of such "anti"- initiatives, these problems have refused to dissolve. They have, for the most part, remained or grown.

The collective human consciousness is beginning to come around to the idea that real change only comes with affirming approaches like positive psychology, mindfulness, building good communication and relationships skills, and health care that fortifies the organism's strengths rather than attacking symptoms of its weaknesses. These kinds of approaches do not require massive amounts of money and are not fueled by anger at circumstances that may or may not shift. Any amount of energy channeled into such approaches bears fruit. It is a slow build, a gentle accumulation of good will that is self-expanding and self-perpetuating.

> *If you want to make peace with your enemy,*
> *you have to work with your enemy.*
> *Then he becomes your partner.*
>
> – Nelson Mandela

Perpetuating conflict, allowing for frozen conflict, and enduring conflict without an eye to repair, limits the growth of individuals and stops the evolution of societies. Ideas born out of peaceful and happy hearts arise from inspiration, not desperation; they look at life through a patient, long view instead of through knee-jerk impulsivity; and they are born from a positive point of view, which taps the brain's powerful resource: creativity.

Solutions that stick take a contemplative, reasoned, positive approach—one that takes place over time, with patience.

We can motivate people through anger and fear for short-term, adrenaline-nursed solutions, or we can learn that mindfully and deliberately creating a desired state has more lasting impact. That movement can begin right now. There is no need to wait for yet another motivating tragedy or for data- driven outcries about injustice.

Peace is a daily, a weekly, a monthly process, gradually changing opinions, slowly eroding old barriers, quietly building new structures.
– John F. Kennedy

Intellectual intelligence—IQ—measures certain created standards of intellectual abilities and is valuable to assess intellectual capacities, but we all know it's possible to be mentally brilliant but emotionally and relationally stunted. EQ measures self-awareness, emotional regulation skills, and one's sensitivity to others; research has clearly demonstrated that EQ is a strong predictor of success and happiness. Its importance has been increasingly appreciated as the need for balance between emotional and intellectual competencies has become evident. EQ is not inborn, but it can be taught through social and emotional learning (SEL) curricula.

I dreamed up PQ—"PeaceQ"—because I saw critical skills still lacking. PeaceQ is a set of learnable skills that promote internal peace, resiliency, harmony, and authentic connections with others as well as facilitating peace in our communities.

When people feel truly at home with themselves and know how to feel balanced and centered within the vicissitudes of life, they are much more helpful to others. When people have relationships where they feel seen, heard, understood and encouraged, and can tell each other the truth with compassion and commitment, PeaceQ can be robustly expressed. When people sit in circles, listening deeply to one another and sharing from their heart about meaningful and diverse topics, PeaceQ is experienced within a vibrant lacework of understanding and togetherness.

PeaceQ skills turn us away from "anti-" perspectives to focus on proactively creating a world where people's fundamental needs to be understood and supported are met. Instead of fighting against problems inside ourselves and with others, we can develop these skills both personally and collectively to come together, uplift ourselves, and inspire others.

If we really want to be change agents, we must be vibrant

examples of such a change. PeaceQ skills are about envisioning that change, then holding intentions and engaging in practices that create what we DO want and further the courageous efforts of others.

People are more calmly and genuinely motivated by their lives being meaningful, loving, and joyful.

Aren't you?

PeaceQ Quiz

This quiz is designed to motivate, celebrate, and reinforce your developing PeaceQ. Take it before diving into this book, and then again after you finish reading it. Each month thereafter, you can retake the quiz to check your process and determine areas that still could use improvement.

Circle the number that best reflects what is true for you for each question. Add up your score and check the key at the bottom to see how you did:

1-Never True

2-Rarely True

3-Sometimes True

4-Mostly True

5-Always True

***

1. I take time each day for quiet reflection. 1 2 3 4 5

2. I exercise every day. 1 2 3 4 5

3. I get to sleep at a reasonable hour. 1 2 3 4 5

4. I express my creativity every day. 1 2 3 4 5

5. I eat healthily every day. 1 2 3 4 5

6. I tell others how much I appreciate them. 1 2 3 4 5

7. I express my gratitude daily. 1 2 3 4 5

8. I am eager to admit my mistakes. 1 2 3 4 5

9. I seek to repair my mistakes. 1 2 3 4 5

10. I talk directly to people I have conflicts with.
1 2 3 4 5

11. I invite others to share their opinions, even when
they differ from mine. 1 2 3 4 5

12. I listen without interrupting. 1 2 3 4 5

13. I am accountable for my mistakes. 1 2 3 4 5

14. I keep my word to others. 1 2 3 4 5

15. I keep my word with things I have promised to do
for myself. 1 2 3 4 5

16. I have healthy ways to express my strong feelings.
1 2 3 4 5

17. I can laugh at my imperfections. 1 2 3 4 5

18. I take a moment to breathe deeply before I respond
to someone's complaint. 1 2 3 4 5

19. I notice my judging thoughts about others and make
an effort to be more accepting and open. 1 2 3 4 5

20. I think about how things must feel to others when
trying to understand them. 1 2 3 4 5

21. I concentrate on the best parts of people and do my
best to bring out the best in people. 1 2 3 4 5

22. I forgive myself quickly and learn from my

mistakes. 1 2 3 4 5

23. I am eager to forgive others, even if I choose not to be around them. 1 2 3 4 5

24. I use words wisely and for highlighting the good of others. 1 2 3 4 5

25. I practice "speaking from my heart." 1 2 3 4 5

26. I practice "listening from my heart." 1 2 3 4 5

27. I practice inviting other people to talk as much as I do. 1 2 3 4 5

28. I spend time putting myself in a positive state of mind. 1 2 3 4 5

29. When someone does something upsetting, I am curious what is going on with them. 1 2 3 4 5

30. When someone uses disrespectful language, I use a lighthearted approach to talking with them about it. 1 2 3 4 5

31. I am open about my ignorance on topics and allow others to know more than me. 1 2 3 4 5

32. I spend time each day practicing some form of mindfulness, training my mind to be more present. 1 2 3 4 5

33. When I am not peaceful in my thoughts, feelings, or actions I know I can learn from that too and begin again. 1 2 3 4 5

34. I can be imperfect and flawed and totally lovable too. 1 2 3 4 5

35. I see others as strong and capable and promote their resilience and capabilities. 1 2 3 4 5

36. I am honest, even when I am scared of the consequences. 1 2 3 4 5

37. People can count on me to do what I say. 1 2 3 4 5

38. I am known for talking about people in the best of ways. 1 2 3 4 5

39. I seek to repair the harms I have caused, big or small. 1 2 3 4 5

40. I actively let others know how they have helped me. 1 2 3 4 5

If you scored 60 or below:
You have a great opportunity to become more competent with your PeaceQ. Take to heart every chapter of this book and practice every day!

If you scored 60-80:
You are on you way to PeaceQ! You'll learn fast if you apply yourself.

If you scored 80-100:
You're mastering PeaceQ. Keep practicing; you are a shining example to others and a force for peace in your world.

If you scored 100-140:
Either PeaceQ is in your bones, or you've been practicing for a long time. You are ready to become a PeaceQ mentor.

If you scored 140-180:
You are a mentor of PeaceQ and deserve lots of gratitude for

bringing the world more peace and happiness.

Also, track your PeaceQ progress by signing up for the PeaceQ website application (see the Appendix on page 149 for details), where you can keep a weekly tally of your efforts and contributions.

May I work each day to increase my PeaceQ.

PeaceQ Working Convictions

Peace is not merely a distant goal that we seek,
but a means by which we arrive at that goal.
— Martin Luther King, Jr.

In its broadest sense, PeaceQ describes our ability to reframe conflict-oriented approaches into positive possibilities. PeaceQ comes with our willingness to drop defensiveness in favor of listening to multiple voices and opinions. It is our commitment to live peaceful lives not just in theory, but also in the way we approach problems and each other.

PeaceQ is built on 10 Working Convictions:

1. **Hold an attitude of gratitude.**
   Think we don't have anything to be grateful for?
   Think again.

2. **Be our word.**
   Honesty is not just a virtue; it is the foundation of trust and authentic connection. We are only as dependable and trustworthy as we are good to our word. The agreements we make with others and ourselves are the bedrock of our character.

   If we are to influence others to be more peaceful, we

need to be models of honesty and reliability. We can only be truly peaceful when we have developed our personal integrity. When our word to others or ourselves is golden, people can depend on us and trust in us. Building mastery of PeaceQ means doing what we say, and being known for keeping our word.

3. **Teach instead of preach.**
   Showing people what we value through our actions is much more impactful than lecturing them about how to be. And the most important example we can set in creating a peaceful world is to care for ourselves well and tenderly. In walking that talk, we set a living, loving example of peace. Others respond best to our loving example of what we believe in.

4. **Seek to understand.**
   Always seek to understand why someone would behave badly. Appeal to that person's high-minded aspects in seeking repair of harm. Spend some time putting yourself in the other's context in order to have compassion for their state of mind and their feelings. If a person cannot refrain from destructive behaviors, it may be necessary to stop interacting with him or her, and they may have to face corrective consequences. Permitting harmful behavior on an ongoing basis is hurtful to both the harming party and the harmed.

5. **Be accountable.**
   We are most effective when we work on ourselves and on our part of any dysfunction or rupture. Look at your own responsibility first instead of looking

for scapegoats or placing blame on others. It is far better to make amends and/or restitution for harm done and restore our relationships and integrity than to endure or levy punishment, separation, or shame. A foundation of connected, loving, accepting relationships greatly improves the effectiveness of repair.

6. **Work together.**
We are much better when we all work together. Collaborating with all members, or their representatives, from our communities makes us stronger and builds the foundation for sharing of PeaceQ. Although it may be tempting to hang out most with those who are most like us, we become much richer when we learn from others who seem most different than us.

7. **Speak with respect and use honorable language.**
Always be willing to learn about, to use, and to help others use more appreciative and desirable language. Learn to do it without being sanctimonious. Own mistakes and repair them when we use language that stereotypes, hurts, blames, or shames others.

8. **Express emotions responsibly.**
We cannot avoid our emotional lives or deny our felt responses to situations. Repression creates internal pressures that lead to either illness or unanticipated outbursts. Our emotions are important signals about our inner lives. We need to avoid acting out intense emotions in rash and reckless ways. Instead, we can learn safe, responsible ways to express and manage

our emotions. Learning and practicing this skill set is a lifelong endeavor for most of us, but every step we take to improve the ability to share our feelings in healthy ways—and to wait till they are fully expressed to make clear decisions—builds our PeaceQ.

9. **Keep the peace.**

Peace that comes through aggressive means is really only a temporary absence of conflict. A show of power on one side has, for the time being, suppressed the fight of the other side. Real peace is achieved by working through conflict until all sides have a sense of investment and representation in the solution. When we use "might as right" we lose connection in favor of compliance. Compliance is a shortsighted solution for ongoing problems. When we take the time to deeply take in the complaints and needs of conflicting parties and work toward a shared solution, we have more lasting agreements and enduring empathy.

10. **Connect with joy, positive possibility, curiosity, and humor.**

We are most magnetic when we are playful, radiant, and authentic. Approaching problems, conflicts, and those who feel "other" with joy and curiosity rather than negativity or judgment is the fastest way to build connected relationship. And who hasn't been rescued from the worst of days by laughter and levity?

Part One

Peace Within Ourselves

The Look of Peace

*When the power of love overcomes the love of
power, the world will know peace.*

– Jimi Hendrix

I just heard an animal activist say that she wanted to "burn
the scrotum" of a man who had badly hurt an animal.

I often hear Republicans or Democrats demonizing the
other party, hurling hostile epithets across the aisle.

How many times have we seen activists and politicians
hammering away about the need for social justice…with a
look of urgent condemnation or rage on their faces?

Peddling hate toward the haters is not the way to peace.

The look of peace is tranquil. Think of images you've seen
of the Virgin Mary, the Buddha, the Dalai Lama, Nelson
Mandela, Maya Angelou, Malala Yousafzai, adorable
kittens, frisky puppies, and the irresistible innocence of
babies.

The face experiencing inner peace is lit up. It is like a planet
surrounded by spacious sky.

Peace doesn't look like vehemence, insistence, rigidity,
or superiority. Peace looks like relaxation, openness,

curiosity, grace, delight, and wonder.

The look on one's face both reveals and dictates one's mood:

If we are frowning, we are unhappy.

If we are scowling, we are angry.

If we are snarling, we are contemptuous.

If we are smiling, we are content.

If we are laughing, we are joyful.

If we are raising our eyes up with a twinkle, we are in wonder.

Moving from aggression to serenity is sometimes as simple as purposefully thinking about something that brings joy and moves a grin to our faces. This unclenches our bodies, opening a closed fist into a gentle invitation, loosening a tightly closed bud into a blooming flower.

Sometimes your joy is the source of your smile, but sometimes your smile can be the source of your joy.

- Thich Nhat Han

We cannot will anyone else to become more calm or receptive; we can, however, shift ourselves to being better bearers of clear, reflecting light.

May I light my face with openness
May I find my inner smile
May I be a face of kindness
that anyone can rest in
even for a while

The Art of Feeling

The best way out is always through.

– Robert Frost

Whatever your emotions and wherever they show up, building PeaceQ is about learning to express them fully and cleanly as they arise.

Feelings are signals about moving toward or away from experiences, things, or people, and we all get these signals more or less constantly. We are feeling-making machines. Babies demonstrate this perfectly. They cry when they are hurt or frustrated; they yell or pound when they are mad; they shiver or shake when they are scared; they spit things out when they are disgusted; and they laugh and smile brightly when they are happy.

As we age, we have a greater capacity to think about our feelings and decide whether to express them or to follow their guidance. Many of us learn to shut down our feelings to avoid negative responses from others. We now know that suppressing emotion is like putting a seal on a running water valve: It causes pressure and erosion. Emotions are meant to flow, and when they don't, they create distress.

PeaceQ asks us to feel what we feel, name what we feel, take full responsibility for what we feel, and find healthy outlets for our feelings, particularly the less pleasant ones like anger, fear, and shame. In order to do this, we need to take time to notice what we feel and how we feel it.

If we do not have healthy outlets we will probably notice ourselves engaged in the following behaviors:

Screaming at others

Hitting others

Self-harm

Swallowing or suppressing feelings with food, drugs, alcohol, another person, screen time, and/or sex

Getting others to feel sorry for you

Getting others to bag on other people

Engaging in bullying or mean behavior

Getting attention from others through highly charged emotional drama

Isolating

Denying that we have feelings at all

Keeping too busy to feel

Lying to avoid feeling

I have watched people go from person to person, substance to substance, all in attempts to run from their pain. The tragedy is that the pain multiplies with every attempt to substitute escape for facing the actual feeling and the underlying cause. The most effective and direct method to solving emotional pain is to feel it, name it, and deal with it.

Practice identifying your emotional state (sad? mad? frustrated? afraid? joyful? anxious?) and employing healthy outlets to help the emotions work their way through you.

That is the only way to be free. Any suppression or projection of difficult feelings will be only a short-term fix—if that.

Healthy outlets:

Cry your heart out; ask that all your sorrow be released and that you become able to find peace in your heart. This works better if someone can just be with you, helping you cry it out, or otherwise commit fully to releasing your sadness.

Find a place to pound on pillows or scream without interrupting anyone else's peace.

Write a rant or song or draw a picture expressing your deep feelings.

Go for a vigorous walk, dance, or workout in order to release pent-up feelings.

Ask others to support you in moving through your feelings and coming up with positive things to do.

Try Resource Tapping, a way of shifting negative states into positive states (described in full on pages 56-58).

If we are overwhelmed or overwrought we may need others to help us do this. A simple "How are you feeling right now?" from another, coupled with a willingness to actually look inside and answer the question honestly, may be all it takes to turn away from unhealthy outlets and toward healthier ways to cope.

A few more pointers on the art of feeling:

All of us have specific situations that trigger our strongest emotional reactions. Sometimes, these situations seem minor to others, who have their own triggers that don't make sense to us at all!

For example: I have a trigger about people being late because my parents were often late to pick me up when I was little and I was dependent on them. Even now, I feel irrationally terrified when someone is late because at some deep level I believe I am being abandoned. Once I realize this, I can comfort my older self by saying, "I am in charge now, and I can leave when I want to," I can soothe myself and not act like a child having a tantrum when someone is late.

Take time to reflect on the triggers you've noticed for yourself and work to free yourself from those triggers.

When you are scared, shake your body out and say the following words: "I am scared, and I am okay." It really helps to give yourself permission to be scared and realize that, in that moment, you are okay. Fear is often predicated on what might happen in the future. Releasing it in the present moment helps you face what is to come with a calmer heart and mind.

Feelings are entirely subjective and, therefore, each

person's universe of feeling is entirely self-created. This is easily demonstrated by the fact that what some people find terribly sad or maddening, others find amusing. For example: I feel sad and mad when people are late to class, but I know many teachers that are late themselves to class and have very loose boundaries with time. I feel so happy when people share their most authentic feelings with me in an open and vulnerable way, but I know many people are frightened of expressed feeling and want to avoid it at all costs.

Practice "owning" your feelings rather than blaming others for your own feeling states. Avoid using the term "You make me feel..."

Let others know how you honestly feel in a vulnerable way, not in a blaming way. Recognize that if you want to complain, what you really want is to make a request. Translate complaints into kind, assertive requests: Instead of "You never call me back!" try "I feel neglected when you do not call back. I would like you to text or call me even if it is to say you won't be able to talk for a period of time."

Make sure you have a number of people to go to when you are upset. Having only one person to rely on is too much pressure for anyone. No one person can meet all your emotional needs. Nor can you be the only one for someone else. The most emotionally healthy people have a list of personal and professional allies who they can call when they need an emotional release.

People with high PeaceQ acknowledge their feelings

and have an ongoing practice for releasing feelings. To the degree we can feel all the hard feelings and release them, we possess a wider, bigger valve through which to experience and express the positive emotions. Feelings are our friends if we have them instead of them having us.

May I feel deeply and release my emotions
And find healthy ways for me to express them all
May I process my feelings responsibly and completely
And create an open gate instead of a wall

Mindfulness

mind·ful·ness ('mīn(d)f(ə)lnəs/), noun.
the quality or state of being conscious or aware
of something; i.e., "their mindfulness of the
wider cinematic tradition." 2. a mental state
achieved by focusing one's awareness on the
present moment, while calmly acknowledging
and accepting one's feelings, thoughts, and bodily
sensations; used as a therapeutic technique.

Taking time to become aware of the moment may seem, at the outset, redundant—even bizarre. Aren't we just doing what we are doing anyway? Yet we know that much of the time, when we are doing one thing, our minds are busy doing something else. As humans we are uniquely capable of being in one place physically while being in many other places mentally.

This peculiarly human habit creates a sense of being nowhere fully; which, in turn, leads many of us to be anxious and worried. Mentally, we remain in the past or future, and we cannot fully absorb the moment.

Mindfulness can come through any activity that works our organs of attention toward one object. Prayer can be a practice of mindfulness if we commit to our prayer even as other thoughts compete or invade. Making art or music can be   a mindful practice if we purposefully bring our attention back to our creative expression even as other distractions beckon.

The simplest form of mindfulness is sitting, standing, or walking quietly and watching the breath as thoughts stream in and out. When we take even 5 to 10 minutes a day to be silent and to witness our breath as it naturally comes in and out of our belly, we become much more able to focus in general.

The mind is like a young puppy. No matter how old we are, our mind loves to romp and wander. Focused attention becomes a loving leash that gently teaches the puppy to calm down and become more disciplined.

Mindfulness has been studied enough that we now know it improves sleep, test scores, mood and attitude. That's a lot of benefit for a practice that takes only 5 to 10 minutes each day.

Here is a short mindfulness meditation many people like to use:

> Sit quietly without any digital or visual distractions. Repeat these phrases while focusing on relaxing your body and letting go of all other concerns:
>
> May I be happy.
>
> May I be well.
>
> May I be safe.
>
> May I be peaceful and at ease.

May you be happy.

May you be well.

May you be safe.

May you be peaceful and at ease.

May we all be happy.

May we all be well.

May we all be safe.

May we all be peaceful and at ease.

You will find, after even just a few minutes, that your well-being is improved and your attitude is set toward more positive possibilities for you and others.

> *May I learn to calm my mind*
> *and learn to focus on being kind*
> *May I cultivate a serene attitude*
> *and benefit from a positive and loving mood*

Keep Your Word To Yourself

When we keep the promises we have made to ourselves we create a vessel of incredible strength and quietude.

Ironically, many of us feel comfortable breaking our word to ourselves—as if we don't count. Most of us break promises to ourselves far more readily than we break promises made to others.

"I will not drink this week."

"I will finish this essay by Sunday."

"I will visit my mother this month."

"I will take a break from eating sweets."

"I will get up earlier and go to the gym."

PeaceQ means realizing that the way we treat ourselves is the strongest possible predictor of the way we live in the world outside ourselves.

If we are faithful, compassionate, and dedicated to the things we know will bring us more health, composure, and joy, we will be a beacon of stillness and support for others and be naturally drawn to nourishing people and experiences.

Exercise:

Each day at a specified time, write out a small promise to yourself. Keep it specific and doable: I will drink three glasses of water during the day; I will take a 20-minute walk this evening; I will tell one person in my life how much I appreciate him or her. At the end of each day, check off that you have done it. Put a star next to it or some symbol of congratulations.

If possible, share this process with a friend; be each other's touchstones for success. Share your success with your friend and hear his or her success too. If you don't make good on your small promise, recommit to doing so the next day.

Simple steps completed create a stairway to self-respect.

Be your word, and your word will set you free.

Reclaiming Resilience

rə'zilyəns/noun
*1. the ability of a substance or object to spring
back into shape; elasticity. 2. the capacity to
recover quickly from difficulties; toughness.*

Resilience is testimony to our evolution and grit. We possess extraordinary genetic adaptability and survival instincts; we can overcome adversity and meet small and big challenges with gusto.

Years ago, I met a young woman named May who had been raped by nine members of her family and their friends throughout her childhood. When she first told me this, I wanted to take her in my arms and never let her into the world again. I wanted to be the emotional shelter she never had.

But I soon recognized that May had not told me this as a victim, but as a proud survivor. "I am so lucky I survived," she told me. "I got out. Now I choose who is close to me, and I choose well." She did not want to be seen as her trauma or her wounds. She wanted to be seen as the heroine she was.

Resilience is based on the notion that we are not what happens to us; we are what we make of what happens to us. A person's outstanding character is not formed by what comes easily, but what a person is able to do despite obstacles or adversity.

When we believe that people are weak, needy, incapable, or inadequate, we may want to rescue them. We may try to lift them out of adversity and provide them with a safe refuge. When we rescue people, we infer that they are helpless or powerless.

> *We're our own dragons as well as our own heroes,*
> *and we have to rescue ourselves from ourselves.*
>
> – Tom Robbins

If someone is drowning, it is appropriate to save him or her. If someone is about to be struck by a car, snatching them out of harm's way is the right thing to do, as long as you're not unduly risking your own safety. When people are a danger to themselves or others they may need to be physically removed from the situation.

But often, we approach perfectly capable people in adverse situations and treat them as though they have no strength. We fail to recognize that they have the capacity to arrive at their own creative solutions.

> *If they hadn't told me I was ugly, I never would have*
> *searched for my beauty. And if they hadn't tried to*
> *break me down, I wouldn't know that I'm unbreakable.*
>
> – Gabourey Sidibe

When I rescue someone from a social or emotional situation without considering his or her choice, decision, or volition in the matter, I imply that:

1. That person is helpless or hopeless in some way.

2. I am that person's savior.

3. That person does not have the internal or external resources or assets he or she needs in order to handle the situation.

Rescuing another from a challenging situation may achieve short-term relief at the expense of the development of long-term emotional strength.

> *You have to believe in yourself when no one else does—that makes you a winner right there.*
> – Venus Williams

Let's say my friend has come to me because she is not being treated well by her boyfriend. This time, she is sure she cannot take it anymore. I agree with her, since I have heard the same story dozens of times from her about this same partner. I figure out how to get her to break up with him and give her truly sage advice about how to move on. She is immediately grateful; I feel proud of my contribution in steering her away from this destructive relationship.

A week later, she is back together with the guy. "I just can't quit him!" she says. I feel like an idiot. She feels my judgment. Now I'm mad at her for being so weak. She's feeling persecuted by me because she is not living up to my standards.

What if I'd asked her about her own sense of things with this guy and how she wanted to handle the situation? If I had reflected her truth and her standards back to her and told her that I was confident that no matter how long it took, she would figure out what to do. I might have been less ego-invested in the outcome. She might have had to work harder to find her own authentic solutions, but those solutions would be hers, and they'd be more likely to stick. She would feel empowered—the captain of her own ship, solving her own problems, and facilitating her own growth trajectory. She develops resilience.

> *I never said I wanted a 'happy' life but an interesting one. From separation and loss, I have learned a lot...We don't even know how strong we are until we are forced to bring that hidden strength forward.*
>
> – Isabel Allende

When we rescue in nonlife and death situations, we create and enable victims. When we focus on the strengths and capacities of each person, and live out the belief that they are their best internal advisors and experts, we can ask helpful questions and respond to reasonable requests. We relate not as a savior or judge, but as an ally.

To highlight others' resilience requires that we scan for their internal and external assets; that we reward their moxie, backbone, and tenacity. We regard them as intrinsically capable people and see them as able to face and overcome adversity.

One press account said I was an overnight success.
I thought: 'That was the longest night I've ever spent!'
– Sandra Cisneros

The opposite of resilience is victimhood and victim thinking. It is blaming others for one's conditions or situations, being frustrated and angry at aspects of our lives that we either cannot control or that we are creating and expanding through our own thinking and choices. A life lived as a victim demonstrates the condition of the mind more often than the ongoing conditions or situations in one's life.

Where there is no struggle, there is no strength.
– Oprah Winfrey

PeaceQ requires that we acknowledge our pain and wounds deeply without pretense, but also that we consider setbacks and injustices as "grist for the mill."

Life is not easy for any of us. But what of that?
We must have perseverance and, above all, confidence
in ourselves. We must believe that we are gifted for
something, and that this thing, at whatever cost,
must be attained.
– Marie Curie

We can only be truly peaceful if we see the potential of injury or trauma to lead us home to our indomitable and capable spirits; as a way to make what we are truly made of more visible, powerful, and of service to others.

May I see the strength in others
And believe they can give their best
May I support them to face their obstacles
Knowing only they can pass their tests

Cultivating Gratitude

A life spent in contemplation of gratitude is a life of incessant heart opening.

Most of us in the developed world know we have lots to be grateful for in a material sense. We know we should be grateful for our loved ones and for precious moments that connect us to people, ideas, and pursuits that matter to us.

We are all more blind to what we have than to what we have not.

– Audre Lorde

Most of us forget sometimes; some of us forget more than others.

Let's look at how a certain kind of gratitude helps build supportive, connected relationships and reduces judgment and prejudice.

We live in a society of superstars, ultimate athletes, billionaire king/queen makers, and the fantasy of being number one. The cost of this is that we have become unaware of how many other people have paved the way for us to do anything we do well.

The myth of the self-made man or woman is just that:

a myth.

Yes, industry, hard work, and self-reliance are virtues of every master in any field, but what is less remarked upon is how many people have helped the lauded few climb to the top. Under any great man or woman is a mountain of doers that support them, often through small or even forgotten actions. Why do we focus on the most sparkly face, ring, or empire while barely seeing the humble entities that keep up the shine on a day-to-day basis?

The culture of competition and superiority does spur on heroic ambition. People who enter the top one percent are covered by media and envied by many. (Envy tends to fall away when these famous people make mistakes and suffer vicious public humiliations.)

This glamorization of the golden few may obscure the kindnesses of strangers or friends who do the simple things in life for others out of generosity of spirit—not because they want anything, but because they wish to give generously and to be part of our lives. They need to be acknowledged and appreciated for their contributions too.

Each one of us wants to be seen for what we offer. Nowadays, with so much economic and social disparity, we can overlook gestures from others if they do not come from a higher-up rung of the ladder. Is it egotistical or small-minded to want our contributions to be noted? No! It's human. Humility is sometimes misunderstood as the self-effacing denial of our strengths or gifts. True humility is accepting our gifts and failings with equanimity, and gracefully receiving feedback on both.

Demonstrating Gratitude

We do not have equal resources or capacities to give material things, but we all do have the need to be recognized for what we do give, within the scope and context of who we are and the skills and resources we possess.

We cannot all give in the same way.

You may be able to host a community event at your beach mansion.

I may be able to load your trash onto your dump truck.

I may be able to give you professional advice on color-coordinating your new place, although my house is a rental with an old, shaggy, smelly cat. (I won't be asking you there.)

You may be able to host me at a gourmet dinner with perfectly paired wines.

I may be able to write you a handwritten note of thanks, which will take me an hour to write because writing is not my thing; I put in the effort because I want you know how much what you did meant to me.

You may go out of your way to host my partner and me at a concert to which you could get special seats.

I may spring for the round of drinks and offer to be

the designated driver…and that is a real reach for me because I love to drink!

You may be able to invite us on a lovely walk through a park.

I may be able to help your daughter get through a really rough time with her breakup because I'm a good listener.

We often overlook the stitching on the dress in favor of the diamond buttons. There would be no diamonds to stare at if the small stitches weren't woven throughout, keeping the garment together! Isn't it funny how often great stitching is cited for being practically invisible?

How hard is it really to notice that everyone, at his or her level, wants to be known? And seen? And appreciated? Don't you want these things for yourself?

A simple solution for advancing PeaceQ is demonstrating gratitude: bridging slight or enormous gaps of social or economic disparity by looking for every single way we can acknowledge someone for his or her effort, time, expertise, skills, and involvement/desire to be part of our lives.

We do not have to be psychic or telepathic to know what sacrifices people are making to give what they give us. We need only to be curious and deeply interested in the ways people give to us constantly, in ways we might not have noticed before.

Let's break it down into three easy steps:

Step One: Recognize that you are blind to many ways

people give to you every day.

Step Two: Become a "giving detective" and see how many ways you can now notice how others give to you.

Step Three: Whenever you notice someone giving you energy, time, expertise, attention, or help, say something about how grateful you are, each and every time.

> *Silent gratitude isn't very much use to anyone.*
> – Gertrude Stein

Although holding an attitude of gratitude on an internal level can increase our positive intentions and behaviors, the expressions of our gratefulness bring out the best in us and everyone else. These recognitions can be understated and subtle: No one likes an inauthentic cheerleader. They are also not about keeping score of who gives what to whom. Rather they reflect a commitment to taking the blinders off to the obvious and stating gratitude in a straightforward, heartfelt way.

I can say with certainty that a day is much better and more vibrant when I am noticed for even the smallest of my earnest efforts or generosities. When you see someone honestly recognized for a small kindness, watch how that person's face relaxes; watch the sparkle arrive in that person's eyes.

Think others already know how much you appreciate them? This is rarely, if ever, true. Besides: No one has ever complained about being excessively genuinely appreciated! More commonly, people feel invisible for their contributions by the people they live with every day, friends they help, people they work with, and society in general.

Expressions of appreciation heal both the recipient and giver. Psychological research suggests that giving such appreciative expressions is highly beneficial (in terms of better immune system function and neurotransmitter balance).

Telling me what you are grateful for about me will remind me, each time, of how much you care for me; and it will encourage me to do the same for you. It will also inspire you to feel better about yourself and about our connection.

Acknowledgement is, by its nature, a win-win proposition.

May I tell you every way you have been kind
And especially notice the smallest of gestures
May I remember to say my gratitude each time
So they are not just buried treasures

Self-Care

*I have come to believe that caring for myself
is not self-indulgent. Caring for myself
is an act of survival.*

– Audre Lorde

A peaceful person is a like a steady stream of fresh water: simple, straightforward, delicious, transparent, and refreshing.

A peaceful person is not dragged up to great heights and down to deep depths by each latest round of personal drama. Peaceful people have the ability to pay attention to the outside world with interest and curiosity because they are not caught up in roller coasters of endless relationship havoc.

Developing PeaceQ is a way into living a centered, serene life. A major aspect of this way of living is to create numerous ways to be peaceful within ourselves. If we fail to do this, we cannot expect to be peaceful with others.

If you are standing in a torrential downpour of rain rife with lightning and thunder, you cannot reasonably expect to stay dry. Similarly, it is unreasonable to want a peaceful world around you if you are in a body that is thundering in perpetual mental, emotional, physical, or spiritual disease. And, unfortunately, most people are run by their moods, their foods, and their broods—by their vices and devices.

Self-care is not a rosy axiom here. It is a fundamental ingredient of living PeaceQ. It involves maintaining a daily practice of healthy eating, exercise, quiet contemplation, creative expression, and authentic and compassionate communication.

Obviously, this means carving out sufficient time to engage in these activities on most days.

"I don't have time for this!" is the most common thing I hear people say about self-care activities. "I'm too busy! I have too much to do! I can't take the time to _____ " (Fill in the blank: meditate, practice yoga, shop for fresh food and cook a nutritious meal, have a deeply intimate and vulnerable conversation.)

Notice how much time people around you—in particular, those who do not engage in healthy self-care—spend on unhealthy activities like:

gossip

mindless screen time

media obsessions

getting high or drunk

spending endless hours trying to fix others

complaining about others

racing around to buy things or seeking constant entertainment eating out

pigging out at home

racing to cosmetic fix appointments

If you see glimmers of yourself here, consider the old, wise saying: "If you don't have time to meditate for five minutes, you should meditate for twenty."

Self-care is vital to being a balanced and healthy human being: a person who has the best possible chance of using his or her faculties for clear, tempered, and loving interactions.

It is not about being perfect or compulsive about these things. How peaceful would that be? Nor is it about controlling anyone else's self-care. It is about a firm, unwavering dedication to becoming the clearest, most loving vessel we can become.

May I choose to take time for joyful self-care
Understanding that how I am stems from this
May I prioritize all things that are good for me
Instilling well-being and bringing lasting bliss

Tapping In

Why do we do this thing called "Tapping"?

Think of tapping as a little nudge to your neural pathways to create a positive state in the brain. You focus on something positive and use an intentional light physical touch to anchor that thought into your sensate experience, and you emphasize the pruning capacities of your mind to select and develop affirmative mental states. It works like taking a gentle hammer and nailing a beautiful frame to the wall. Your mind becomes a more positive frame to contain ideas and feelings. Your frame of mind has everything to do with how you experience your life. Tapping is a simple technique that stimulates your positive mental and emotional tendencies. The more you practice this technique, the stronger your habit will be to focus on the positive and to scan your life for favorable experiences, people, and mental states.

Self-care through tapping can be extraordinarily simple. On a day when you feel challenged and cranky, taking a simple, brief step to improve your mood and attitude can make all the difference. As you care for yourself in this way, you make yourself more available to collaborate and perform thoughtful deeds for others.

1. Find a comfortable place to sit or lie, where you will not be disturbed. Close your eyes.

2. Take several long, slow breaths, filling the belly, and exhaling slowly. Let yourself relax.

3. Imagine any type of positive state: being peaceful, happy, inspired, motivated, or laughing. This can be called up based on your actual experience—somewhere you've been, or an event from your past—or can be drawn from your imagination as an experience you wish to have. (An imagined experience, seen in detail, can have just as much positive impact as a real one!)

   Once you have an association, bring up as much sensory detail as you can: sights, sounds, smells, sensations, and the emotional feeling that goes with being there. You might even imagine the time of year, the time of day, and what you are wearing in this special place. Check in to feel where in your body you most experience this image, feeling, or sound.

4. When you have a sense of the place, begin to tap on your knees right-left, right-left. The taps can be quick or slow; just find a speed that feels good to you. Do this 6 to 12 times (tapping right and left equals one time). Alternatively, you can do "butterfly taps," crossing your arms in front of your chest and tapping your right upper arm with your left hand and your left upper arm with your right hand.

5. Pause; check in with yourself to see how you are feeling.

6. You may keep tapping as long as it feels positive. Repeat as often as you like.

If you have any question about these instructions above, search for "Laurel Parnell Resource Tapping" on YouTube.

Suggested Positive States for Tapping

Happily surprised

Motivated

Comforted by someone

Excited

Grateful

Cared about

Inspired

Laughing hard

Doing something brave

Completing something you worked hard at

Feeling really relaxed

Feeling open to a new experience

Something really good has just happened

Loving an animal or something in nature

Doing something wonderful for someone – even a small thing

Receiving a gift you loved

Being listened to

Self-Care and Sleep

*Each night, when I go to sleep, I die. And the next
morning, when I wake up, I am reborn.*

– Mahatma Gandhi

Sleep is the prerequisite to renewal. Show me a cranky
human and quite likely I'll show you a person who is not
getting enough sleep. Some of us don't sleep as well as
others, but all of us (aside from those who work the night
shift, or those with young children) have a choice in terms
of how and when we get to sleep at night.

Despite a general understanding that good solid sleep is
necessary, many of us deny ourselves the sleep we need.
Without sleep, we can't be at the top of our game. We all
know from experience how crummy a sleep-deprived day
feels. Perhaps we are grasping for some extra fun in those
late hours; perhaps we are numbing out on TV or movies
or surfing the Internet. Whatever it is we're doing when
we could be heading off to dreamland, it's just not worth
it if we aren't getting enough rest.

The art of PeaceQ involves crafting a schedule that
provides enough rest. We'll all have our share of sleepless
nights when emergencies or nerves overcome us. The rest
of the time, we are responsible for bringing much-needed

stillness and lights-out to our weary minds and bodies. With adequate sleep, we think more clearly and have quicker reflexes. We focus better and are more relaxed.

An easy way to add harmony to your life is to bring yourself in balance with a reasonable sleep time. Create a bedtime routine free of digital devices; they actually mess with the calming brain waves characteristic of the moments before sleep.

PeaceQ means dedicating yourself to a life of vigorous activity and service during the day, and sacred, undisturbed rest at night. When you are well rested after a solid night's sleep, you and your reignited zest for life can comfort others. Peace in equals peace out.

May I plan a good night's sleep
as that will be the calm I keep
May I awake to the day full of rest
So I will be giving my best

Exercise:

Apply these guidelines for great sleep preparation:

• Turn off all devices at least two hours before bed.

• Do a calming activity before putting your head on your pillow: reading something calming, knitting, quiet reflection, drawing, journal writing by hand.

• Make a mental list or say out loud verbally all the things and people you are grateful for.

• When you lie down, notice every part of your body

relaxing and thank each part of your body for functioning as well as it does.

- ZZZZZZZZzzzzzzzzzzzz...

Self-Care and Eating Well

One cannot think well, love well, sleep well if one has not dined well.

– Virginia Woolf

When we eat or drink with the aims of clarity and nutritional balance, we feel our best. All of us know that when we eat foods and drink drinks that promote strong, calm, and sustained energy, we feel good.

What we put into our mouths influences what comes out of our mouths. When we succumb to foods or drinks that are nutritionally unhealthy, we are much more prone to acting irritably and saying unthoughtful things. Filling our bodies with junk food, drink, or drugs makes us less vibrant and less effective—and, let's admit it, may well make us snarky or bitter. Eating a diet laden with sugar, caffeine, stimulants, and depressants ties us to an emotional roller coaster and imbalanced behaviors.

PeaceQ asks that you consume food and drink that calm the body and mind, help you rest, and steady your deeds and speech.

"We are what we eat" is an old adage. As with most old adages, we hear it often enough that we don't appreciate its depth and applicability even to our modern lives.

Tell me what you eat, and I will tell you who you are.
–Brillat-Savarin

Exercise:

Each day, pick a food or drink that you may be struggling with and want to have a clearer relationship with, in terms of how you actually feel when you have it.

When you eat or imbibe this food or drink, notice how it feels to slow down the entire process of taking it in. Pay close attention to what you are feeling and thinking before, during, and after ingesting it. Notice the immediate effects of this substance on your mood, attitude, and physical energy, both at the moment you take it in and for the hours following. Pay attention to short-term gains and long-term consequences.

Let's take coffee as an example. Let's say that what's true about coffee for me is also true for you: You notice a big zip in energy and sometimes irritability, followed about two hours later by a little crash.

Ask yourself the question: "How would I be if I could never have this again in my life?" Notice all the emotions that come up in response.

Then, ask yourself the questions: "How is this substance helping me?"

"Could I get the positive attributes I receive from it without any negatives?"

"Is there anything else that would be better for me to

choose that would have only positive benefits?"

Finally: Notice whether this substance choice is emotional or nutritional.

May I eat what helps me thrive
helping my mind and body feel most alive
May I be conscious of my food and drink decisions
celebrating the power of clean and healthy living

Creativity

Every child is an artist. The problem is how to remain an artist once he (she) grows up.

– Pablo Picasso

A young woman of 15 named Emilika said to me one day, "When you feel like hate...just create!"

She understood that the big gift we all have at our disposals, in any given moment, is imagination. No one has control over what we can dream up or imagine.

If we spent less time being sucked in by visual entertainment on the Internet, we would have more time to play with the biggest canvas ever: the unlimited landscapes of our imaginations.

I often hear people say, "I have no imagination!" or "I'm not creative." How sad a thing to hear: Someone, once, or repeatedly, must have given this message to that person. Now, chained to that belief, she denies herself the joy and healing power of creative imaginings and expression.

To form something out of nothing can happen every day in abundance, and so many variations on this theme are possible!

My friend Marla creates extraordinary dinner parties

with themes.

My friend Stacy riffs on ideas to change education.

My friend Roxy makes gorgeous flower bouquets to brighten people's lives when they are having a rough time.

My friend Jerry brings his dog to the hospital to bring smiles to patients' faces.

My beloved Rendy creates stupendous menus for meals and makes them regularly for friends and family.

My friend Aida cleans houses with a special touch of making beautiful arrangements of things.

My friend Nina has a treasure trove of costume feline tails she collects and wears.

My friend Debbie is an expert at putting thrift store clothes together into high-style outfits.

True regenerative power is nestled in with imagination and the ability to creatively express one's self. The people I know who spend their days in active and fruitful creativity are never concerned with dominating others because they feel the embrace of the universe flowing through them in their art form or inventive expression. When you feel that kind of inspiring flow of energy, you never have to push your agenda on anyone because you already feel so fulfilled.

You see things; and you say, "Why?" But I dream things that never were, and I say, "Why not?"
— George Bernard Shaw

In many cases, we have given up our right to create to people who are good at it or who can make money at it. Many of us have been tortured by the false idea that we need to have "talent" to express ourselves. We have forfeited one of the most fundamental joys of being human: the making of things, or making things up, for fun.

The key is to know that every one of us can tap into this kind of energy by taking the time to do something generative every day. Singing, dancing, writing, playing an instrument, drawing, or other art forms are not just the province of professionals! Take money, approval, and/or recognition off the table, and you can play like a free child with your imagination. Take the ruthless critic out of the room and the fun can really get started.

Think left and think right. Think low and think high. Oh, the thinks you can think up if only you try!
– Dr. Seuss

No one has ever suffered from cavorting with writing, dancing, painting, taking photographs, or playing music for their own pleasure! If you can walk, you can dance. If you can talk, you can sing. If you can write at all, you can write a poem, a book, or a screenplay. Try collage, building with blocks, rapping, drumming, making up some choreography to your favorite song—whatever engages your creative gears! You can do pretty much anything you can think of for creative self-expression if you do not need the resulting product to be "good." The process of expression is far more important than the product.

We all have been given this priceless gift of being able to bring our imagination into form. Many of us have come to believe that we can't open this gift for ourselves until someone outside of us begs us to do so, or until someone puts a price tag on it. An appreciation of creative expression in ourselves and in others brings lightness to our communities and is a vital aspect of celebrating our right to joy and play.

Exercise:

Ignite your playful creativity! Do this alone, or with others.

1. Pick any object you see: i.e., the lamp.
2. Give that object a silly name: i.e., Hairy Fairy.
3. Give that object a funny voice: i.e., tiny mouse voice.
4. Have that object—in our example, the lamp named Hairy Fairy with the tiny mouse voice— narrate observations of what that lamp sees, out loud or in writing.

Notice how the act of being creative gets you out of a fixed mindset and into a more pliable, open state of mind.

Remember to LAUGH!!

May I take time today to expressively create and
find wonder in something I make
May I remember the beauty in simple play
And revel in acts of
imagination each and every day

Reappraising Prejudgments

When we can stop our involuntary assessments of others—those assumptions that make an "ass" out of "u" and "me"—and, instead, steer our brains toward the best possible appraisal of another, we can live in a much richer and more varied social world.

We all make up stories and hold assumptions about others based on skin color, class, voice, posture, looks, and other external factors. The brain is wired to prejudge; this has survival value, as it helps us discern self from other and potential enemy from friend.

At the root of this instinctive tendency to stereotype others is the tribal instinct to categorize: *To whom do I belong? Who has my back? Who is going to threaten me?*

Prejudice is a burden that confuses the past, threatens the future and renders the present inaccessible.

– Maya Angelou

What is hilarious is that our brains fire so differently that what or who looks scary to you could read to me as someone safe enough to be my best friend. I see a policeman and think, "There is a great, kind officer who is here to protect me." My friend Gera sees a police officer and thinks, "There is someone who wears the same uniform as the people who beat up my cousin for no reason. I hate them."

Prejudging is based on historic experiences and fearful attitudes that are then generalized to stereotypes. Sometimes prejudgments are a result of ignorance and lack of experience, combined with prejudices held at the level of societies or passed on from generation to generation.

None of us are exempt from other people's judgments. None of us can control this initial instinct to judge others; it's part of our legacy as humans who once had to make much faster assessments to stay alive and be able to pass on our DNA. In this age, PeaceQ requires that we step back from our involuntary associations and judgments and consider that they just may not be true. We can consciously bring in PeaceQ thoughts: shifting an impulse from prejudgment toward curiosity and the assumption that most people, most of the time, are doing the best they can to be good and helpful.

Let the first thought come in and accept that it is driven by conditioning and instinct. Then, let a PeaceQ thought bubble up from a space of curiosity and willingness to connect.

For example:

I see an enormous man get out of a black SUV that just cut me off to get a parking space.

First thought: "That entitled pig thinks he's better than me!"

PeaceQ thought: "I wonder what is going on with this guy that he's in such a hurry?"

I see a homeless woman pushing a cart down the street.

First thought: "Is she an addict?"

PeaceQ thought: "How is she doing? How can I be kind and compassionate to her?"

Notice that the first involuntary thoughts here are not pleasant. They create separation and righteousness. Both these states are stressful to the body and mind. Conversely, the PeaceQ thought calms the nervous system and offers an opportunity for peace between us.

Prejudging is not always a negative stereotype and sometimes can be quite the opposite; however, any blind appraisal is still limited.

I see a young man who is totally buff and dressed impeccably.

First thought: "He is so hot and successful."

PeaceQ thought: "I wonder how he's feeling and what his life is like?"

I see a movie star having lunch at the table across from me.

First thought: "I wish I could be that person. She has everything she could ever want."

PeaceQ thought: "There is a person who is constantly stared at. I wonder how it is for her to have such a public life?"

These first thoughts might seem positive at the outset, but they are superficial assessments that miss the interior. They, too, create separation and objectification.

PeaceQ thoughts create more interest in the actual, living, breathing person in front of you than in their surface attributes. Such thoughts allow us to feel empathy instead of false idealization or knee-jerk condemnation.

PeaceQ recognizes that we all are wired to prejudge, and that an active interest in harmony and interconnectedness and an appreciation of difference are required to work through the initial filters through which we may see the world.

In our work and in our living, we must recognize that difference is a reason for celebration and growth, rather than a reason for destruction.
– Audre Lorde

It takes but a beat, a breath, and a questioning of our assumptions that come from a head space that feeds off division and compartmentalization to move into a heart space that is peaceful and accepting.

May I notice when I prejudge
failing to see clearly
May I yearn to truly know another
and hold their differences, like my own, dearly

Embracing Honesty

When we have an honest relationship with someone, we feel solid inside and fortified to meet the world. When we know someone else counts on our veracity, we feel important and trusted.

A lie, by its very nature, destabilizes everyone that lie impacts, including the one who has lied.

> *When we discover that someone we trusted can be trusted no longer, it forces us to reexamine the universe, to question the whole instinct and concept of trust. For a while, we are thrust back onto some bleak, jutting ledge, in a dark pierced by sheets of fire, swept by sheets of rain, in a world before kinship, or naming, or tenderness exist; we are brought close to formlessness.*
> — Adrienne Rich,
> Women and Honor: Notes on Lying

How can we have equanimity, or peace internally, if we are lying? To the degree we harbor secrets or deceive others and ourselves, we live in disharmony and shame.

We may all agree on the surface that it is not good to lie; however, not one among us has failed to find rationalizations for telling untruths both small and enormous. Some of us have been so traumatized that we have learned to live in denial of truths and need professional help to feel safe enough to acknowledge truths honestly and to deal with them. Some of us have become so numb that we have temporarily lost the capacity to know what we feel, and need a guide to gently help us enter back to the world of feeling.

When I was small, my mother used to drum into me how bad it was to lie. And then, I would watch her answer the phone in a perky voice just following a blood-curdling fight with my father. "I'm great!" she'd chirp. It disturbed me to see such a blatant denial of how she was really feeling.

On other occasions, I would hear her say she couldn't go somewhere because she was busy with work. I knew this too was a lie.

We all are tempted to lie for convenience, to avoid anger, to cover up our errors, and to hide our flaws. A booming plastic surgery industry testifies to our desire to cover up our actual ages and natural features in favor of younger, lifted appearances.

Lies are everywhere. Every day, they erode our sense of reality and safety. When we travel in the company of lies, we are instinctively anxious.

We might ask: If everyone is lying, even just a little, why should it matter if we do it too?

PeaceQ maintains, contrary to popular belief, that there is no such thing as an undamaging lie. PeaceQ asks us to rise above the prevailing norms of "white lies," harmless omissions, and those lies we tell to try to avoid hurting someone's feelings.

> *No legacy is so rich as Honesty.*
>
> – William Shakespeare,
> All's Well That Ends Well, Act 3, Scene 5

To obtain peace within, and to have any reasonable hope of helping others find peace, we need to be ardently authentic: being willing to speak inconvenient truths. This does not mean "honesty at all costs," which some people interpret as the permission to be unkind and merciless in speech. I might have the opinion that your hairdo is hideous, but someone else might like it just fine. My failing to share this dislike with you isn't a lie, unless you ask me what I think of it. I can keep an opinion or a judgment to myself and still be walking in truth.

But let's say we are supposed to meet for lunch, and I do not want to go because your loud voice embarrasses me. If I tell you that I can't meet you for lunch because I have a stomachache…that is a lie.

Telling the truth is not about inflicting pain by blurting negative thoughts or opinions out loud. That is just rudeness. Truth telling is about sharing openly regarding anything that has to do with our trusting each other, and about the upholding of the dependable realities that our words and deeds construct.

The art of practicing PeaceQ confirms that we are responsible to first admit to ourselves the things we wish were not true, and to then speak to others from a compassionate and tender place of humility and honesty. All of us can become much more proficient at revealing the truth: from the smallest of lies ("I'll be there in 5 minutes," when you mean 15) to the biggest whoppers (Bill Clinton's "I did not have sex with that woman").

The only way we can elevate other people's behavior in this area is to be an example ourselves. PeaceQ reminds us that it is not our job to take inventory on other people's progress in becoming more truthful; we have enough detailed self-reflection to do on our ends. If I have the courage to tell you hard truths in a soft, caring way— especially if they involve sharing my own weaknesses— you will   see that underlying any real sharing of truth is a commitment to peace and love.

> *May I be free to know my truths are good enough*
> *Even when lying seems easier and things are rough*
> *May I be loved for who I truly am*
> *Without pretense, hiding, or running a scam*

Leading with Love, Happiness, and Peace

No one will dispute that people who lead with love, happiness, and peace are deeply cherished. But our Western culture prizes fame, money, and power (FMP), the pursuit of which has led many a fine person into corruption, lying, deceit, greed, and sometimes even violence.

We all have been led to believe that if we have one or all of these three, fame, money, or power, that we will be loved, happy, and peaceful (LHP). The irony is that the acquisition of fame, money, or power rarely, if ever, changes anyone's capacity for love, happiness, or peace.

Every day we read about ascents to fame, money, and power, and the extravagance of those who seem to "have it all." We also hear daily about people starving, homeless, and without adequate education or medical care. Both ends of the spectrum are seriously out of balance.

> *Wealth consists not in having great possessions,*
> *but in having few wants.*
>
> – Epictetus

I have been honored to work with the poorest youth in our country, some homeless and others without food. I have also been fortunate to work in private practice with some of the wealthiest people in our country.

In one afternoon, I might hear from a young man from a desperately poor family who has just been roughed up by drug dealers; that evening, in my private office, I might talk to someone who is getting ulcers deciding whether or not to buy his third house because the location might not be just right. In the 20 years I have lived in this split world, I have heard and seen the vicissitudes of both poverty and hardship and unimaginable wealth and privilege.

I realize that my particular experience is not statistically valid; however, I can tell you that I have never met an ultra-rich person whose possessions, fame, or power has brought them peace. In fact, I have seen firsthand how much pressure and complexity is added to one's life with the addition of more money, attention, and/or responsibility.

For example: I met a man a few years back who was in knots because he could not stand to settle for just $40 million in his business sale agreement. He spent over a year in agony, feeling like he could not go on unless he had the $20 million more he felt he was due. He became agitated and ill, lost weight, and had horrible fights with everyone around him. He lived a terribly impoverished existence, even though he was one the wealthiest people I knew.

Money often costs too much.
– Ralph Waldo Emerson

PeaceQ means recognizing that having is not as rewarding as *sharing* or *giving*. It takes an active resistance to the culture at large to prioritize *empathy* for others rather than the pursuit of *fame*, *money*, and *power*.

PeaceQ emphasizes a direct route to love, happiness, and peace. If you want to truly be loved, be loving—without an agenda or goal. If you want to sustain and enjoy happiness, be grateful and generous, no matter what your material conditions are. If you want to be peaceful, be at peace with yourself and extend that calmness to others.

The people I know who are loved, happy, and peaceful are people who practice certain skills daily. Use this list as your checklist and add other ideas you have that enhance LHP.

1. Be kind to others.

2. Share help and resources.

3. Sparkle with appreciations of everyone you encounter.

4. Spend time cultivating a quiet and focused mind.

5. Take impeccable care of your body.

6. Be profoundly grateful for whatever you have, and take note of it as often as possible.

7. Have a robust sense of humor.

8. Do not blame or criticize others for your inevitable setbacks and disappointments.

9. Release any agenda you hold about achieving FMP.

10. Accept reality as it is instead of wishing things were different.

Wouldn't it be amazing if we all started shifting our cultural obsessions from FMP to a collective valuing of LHP?

What a difference it could be: to grow up striving to be loving, happy, and peaceful rather than famous, rich, or powerful. What a leap in the evolution of consciousness it would be to educate our children from birth in cultivating a peaceful, happy heart.

May I cherish love, happiness, and peace
for that is what really feeds me
May I let go of the drive for money, fame, and power
for that is what deludes me

Connect With Curiosity and Humor

It is a curious fact that people are never so trivial as when they take themselves seriously.

– Oscar Wilde

In our human evolution, we have spent thousands of years in conflicted, non-collaborative paradigms. The quantum leap out of this fisted approach is more essential than the next iteration of computers, power, software, robots, or space travel.

The simple practices and concepts required for this leap are as obvious and radical as those that went into the invention of the light bulb.

Curiosity is a willing, a proud, an eager confession of ignorance.

– Leonard Rubinstein

Comedy is acting out optimism.

– Robin Williams

Our complex modern brains house a smaller, much more primitive reptilian brain that is wired for aggression and defensiveness. Tapping the higher brain when the reptilian brain tries to run the show – which it often does – is a lot easier when we have a sense of humor about this whole thing.

When humor goes, there goes civilization.
– Erma Bombeck

You'll never get to a place where this isn't a struggle. I, for example, was on my way to work, where I planned to talk to my editor about this book. On my way to preach peace and equanimity, I got cut off and yelled "Dumbass!" at the other driver. And not more than a day before that, my partner forgot something I said…and I acted as if she had completely invalidated my existence. I didn't have a sense of humor then! My lizard brain had taken over.

But the more I'm able to joke about it – which, now, I'm able to do minutes later, instead of hours or days as it used to be – the sooner I get back to my higher self, which can understand that the "dumbass" might have been in a huge hurry, just as I've been so often myself while driving; and that my partner had just had a busy day and could hardly remember what she'd come into the kitchen for, much less something I said in passing the day before.

Laugh as much as possible; always laugh. It's the sweetest thing one can do for oneself & one's fellow human beings.
– Maya Angelou

Every human being is working on this, and we all have so far to go: it's one step forward, five steps back. But we should never lose sight of the fact that this is worth the long-term haul.

What other choice do we have in a world riddled with intense and awful conflicts? In a world we might destroy because we have failed to develop empathy for each other as well as the earth itself? Let's not beat ourselves up about all this. Let's see if we can cultivate a great curiosity and sense of humor about how developmentally delayed we are in the concepts of PeaceQ!

Exercise:

A simple humor exercise you can do alone or with others:

Take a situation in your life that feels difficult, and that you have talked about or thought about a lot; something you are already a little tired of focusing on.

Pick a cartoon voice or character that is a little absurd.

Tell your situation as if you were this cartoon character. Make sure to exaggerate the voice and gestures!

Let yourself become fully ensconced in the extreme comic version of the story.

In poking fun at our dilemmas, we are not invalidating their importance; we are simply loosening the handcuffs of solemnity and tension, both of which inhibit clear thinking.

May I learn to laugh easily
Especially at my own foibles
May I develop an outstanding sense of humor
Sharing that with others as often as I am able

Part Two

Peace With Others

As we practice cultivating peace within, we can simultaneously develop skills and methods to have more peace with others.

There is no solace in perfecting ourselves only to be isolated and alone. We are on this earth with the multitudes. Our most precious moments are often spent in exquisite connection with another or just a close few. The most satisfied people I know are people who love their close others through thick and thin, high and low, and feel that their bonds grow more beautiful, luscious, and dimensional with the test of time. To have this level of fulfillment, one needs to continuously be interested in expanding one's own peace with others.

Practicing a peaceful heart, a peaceful mind, peaceful words, and peaceful actions with others creates a happy you and me.

Each One Teach One

Integrity is congruence between what you know,
what you profess, and what you do.

- Nathaniel Brandon

Empowering and demonstrating to people the actual skills they need to flourish is the surest way to ensure a fulfilling life. On the other hand, if we model ineffective ways to deal with stress or challenges, we pass on inadequacy.

My mother used to say to me, "Do as I say, not as I do," which was terribly confusing. Children learn most deeply by observing the actions of the adults in their lives—the examples they set through their actions and responses. When their words run against the current of those actions and responses, children feel that friction and then live it out in their own lives.

Many of us were raised by people who did not practice what they preached. It is such a temptation to fix the "out-there" and admonish others for their faux pas instead of working on the important scaffolding of our own development. It is tempting to think, "THEY should be more peaceful!" But we cannot work on others to be a way we are not; and I have never met anyone who enjoys being corrected.

How adults often do this:

Drinking a martini while telling their kids not to get high.

Telling young people they have to go to college, even as college becomes unaffordable for most.

Yelling at youth for being on their computers too much, even as they hone their skills at simultaneous texting and yelling.

Demanding that brothers and sisters get along, even as the parents themselves hardly make time to communicate with each other.

Telling youth they have to get their rest, even as many adults are using some kind of stimulant just to get through the day.

Asking, "Why are kids so anxious these days?" while somehow not noticing that adults are self-medicating and running around at a manic pace.

Give a man a fish and you feed him for a day; teach a man to fish and you feed him for a lifetime.

– Maimonides

The idea of "each one teach one" is dramatically different from the dispensing of advice.

It is about directly passing our practiced skills and wisdom on to others by embodying and practicing them—rather than preaching to others what they should know or what they should do.

If I have learned how to change a tire, I can show you how.

If I have learned how to be sober, I can support you, if you want to learn how to be sober.

If I have learned how to manage my anger and not lash out at others, and you want to do that too, I can share what helped me get there.

If I have learned how to repair my mistakes with others by taking full responsibility for my wrongdoings, I can now demonstrate that to you.

If I have learned to eat for vibrant vitality purposes only, then I can work with you on learning to eat more healthfully.

If I have learned how to live within my means and balance my budget, I can explain to you how that works for me.

Exercise:

Make a list of even the simplest skills you possess: i.e., folding laundry, whistling, combing a cat, balancing a checkbook.

Write down next to each skill someone who may benefit from learning that skill.

Make a commitment to teach at least one person a skill you know once a week for a month.

Mentorship is actually the most direct way to affirming your usefulness and roles in this world. Passing on a skill is a direct and pleasurable transmission of peace in action.

May I share what I know with patience and grace
Teaching others to be competent and to do
May I relinquish hypocrisy as it arises
And return to being an avid learner too

Emphasizing Empathy

Sympathy is a necessary handkerchief when others have suffered and you truly feel sorry for them. Empathy, on the other hand, is understanding another person's experience from his or her point of view, feelings, and walk of life.

You think your pain and your heartbreak are unprecedented in the history of the world, but then you read. It was books that taught me that the things that tormented me most were the very things that connected me with all the people who were alive, or who had ever been alive.

– James Baldwin

If someone comes to you and says, "One of my trusted friends just embezzled tons of money from me," you might say, "I am so sorry that has happened to you." That would be sympathy—a perfectly kind response.

If, however, you really imagined what it would be like to have a trusted friend take your money in a fraudulent way and felt it in your own body, and then you let your communication about that come from that emotionally attuned place, you might say something like this: "Wow! That might feel like you have been raped or violated.

You trusted someone, and they used that trust to take something really precious from you." That would be empathy.

Empathy is not reading someone's mind or "getting" exactly what he or she is feeling. It is the longing to connect with something inside of that person's particular world. It is a quest to affirm someone else's inner experience and to link yourself to it.

You can never go wrong if you are curious with your empathy instead of insistent. If someone confides in you that they are thinking of leaving their mate, and you say, "That must make you feel so guilty and ashamed!" and they say, "No, actually I am feeling liberated and hopeful," you would be invited to say, "Oh, I see. This is something you are excited about...it gives you a new-start-in-life feeling."

If you were not empathic you might say, "Well, I'd think you would be feeling some guilt," or something else that "should" the other person. No one likes to be told how to feel; emotional reactions are intensely personal and precious. Empathy improves relationships by replacing judgment and unrequested advice-giving with connection in the moment. The person being empathized with feels truly seen and resonated with, and is not likely to behave reactively toward the person who is offering the empathic response.

PeaceQ practice is not about moralizing, evangelizing, or shaping people in our ideal image of them. It is about creating more understanding, less judgment, and the possibility that even with vast differences, we can find a way to harmoniously relate to one another.

> *All I ever wanted was to reach out and touch*
> *another human being; not just with my hands,*
> *but with my heart.*
>
> – Tahereh Mafi, *Shatter Me*

Empathy is the beginning of the eradication of oppositional conflict. If I dare to imagine what you feel, to understand you from your side of things, and even (for a moment) slip into your shoes exactly the way they fit you, I have put myself   on the road to being united with you. This does not mean I lose my footing or personal interests; it simply softens the hard line boundaries of the ego and illuminates the places where we are all in this topsy-turvy life together. Once I have crossed over into the world as you see and feel it, I can't maintain an isolationist perspective in my dealings with you.

If we truly desire peace with others, we need to move past our convictions of how things are and share in each other's worlds of emotion and thought. In that field of feeling, we become increasingly tolerant of the complexities of our differences.

> *May I be open to feel what you might be going through*
> *and let your feet dangle with mine*
> *May I see things from your point of view*
> *and let my rigid way of how it is unwind*

Be Your Word

I am not bound to win, but I am bound to be true.
I am not bound to succeed, but I am bound to live
up to what light I have.

– Abraham Lincoln

People always ask me, "How do I become more confident?"

The answer is quite simple: Be your word.

Confidence, like peace, begins on the inside, and then expands outward.

The words we choose to speak out loud to others are the foundations from which our relationships are built. They have tremendous power and consequence.

If I say:

> "I'll be there at 2 PM."

> "I will get this letter to you by Wednesday."

> "I am committed to you and only you."

> "We will only go to war if we find weapons of mass destruction."

…these words have intrinsic weight that either build our character and confidence (when they are fulfilled), or undermine our character and confidence (when they are not).

When we do what we say, we build a serene, unshakable foundation upon which others can depend.

Yes: We have the freedom and the right to change our minds and adjust our expectations. If we want to be peaceful, we need a certain amount of flexibility to flow with life instead of becoming rigid and righteous. People with stellar character and authentic confidence do this by renegotiating expectations with people before they break their word.

But many people rationalize not keeping their word by acting as though their word is only valid if other conditions don't intercede:

"I would have gotten here at 2 PM...except I got an urgent call from a friend."

"I couldn't get the letter done by Wednesday because someone didn't get back to me."

"I would have been faithful to you if you had been paying more attention to our relationship."

"We couldn't wait on final confirmation of WMDs... we had to go with the intelligence we were given."

Trust, and therefore peace, is built upon the veracity and reliability of our agreements. We are as solid, or as wobbly, as the ratio of our spoken word to our done deeds. When we consistently break our word we become unreliable and may lose respect from others. People may love us because we are adorable, charming, generous, charismatic, and spontaneous, but if we do not keep our word, they will not trust us. They will not feel peaceful around us.

Peacefulness comes from a calm center unmoved by novelty, distraction, seduction, or rationalization. PeaceQ means being a safe harbor where people know that compassion is anchored deeply there. Most important: We can only become more confident and assured of peace within when we keep our word to ourselves and hold true to our stated values and goals. When we break our word routinely, we feel fragmented internally.

We are as we speak. We are as we do. Our self-images are shaped by a combination of what we declare to others, promises we make to ourselves, and what agreements we actually keep. Showing up when you say you will, no matter what, is an essential element of a satisfying and emotionally successful life.

If I agree to do something and I fail to do it
I become less than my word and my integrity is frayed
If I do what I promise
I become more than my word
I am someone you can trust to do what I say

Repairing Our Word

Everything will line up perfectly when knowing and living the truth becomes more important than looking good.
– Alan Cohen

Since integrity is something we are continually building, we need to be both committed to being our word and non-defensive when we occasionally, and humanly, mess up and break our word.

The art of peace, in this case, is about our willingness to repair the broken agreement, to take full responsibility without elaborate excuses, and to begin again in earnest to restore our integrity. The more quickly we repair our breaches, and the more masterful we become at keeping our word, the more calm and available to others we will be.

Exercise:

Find three small examples in the last month of not keeping your word. Make sure these are very small infractions so that you can do the repair easily.

i.e., I said I would not put wet towels on the wood table, and I did.

i.e., I said I would call L. back about reviewing her work on the manual. We did not set a deadline; however, I still have not even called.

Ask the person you broke your word with if he or she has time for a small chat or a phone call.

When you talk, begin with, "I want to repair a broken agreement with you that is entirely my responsibility." Then, speak in brief and accountable language, without excuses: "You had asked me not to put wet towels on the wood. I did it unconsciously and broke my agreement with you. This must have sucked for you, and I want to tell you I feel badly about it. I would like to do something like dust all the wood on Saturday, if that works for you."

Listen to the person's feelings and wait to see if they have a request. Then, ask: "Are we complete on this?" If the answer is "yes," hooray! If the answer is "no" or "not yet," continue the dialogue until resolution.

> *May I be humble when I mess up*
> *Able to say, "it's my mistake"*
> *May I quickly find a way to repair*
> *And be willing to do what it take*

Celebrating What You Don't Know

No one on this planet knows everything. "Beginner's mind" is an attitude of always being willing to learn anew, even in situations where you have incredible experience or expertise. Being open to learning—to entertaining complex and diverse thoughts—and willingness to not know is the road to peace of mind.

People who are certain can be certain of only one thing: They will only be happy if others agree with or defer to them. Someone who postures as the knower above others inherently creates a hierarchy of knowledge and a ladder of unequal worth for ideas.

> *You have your way. I have my way. As for the right way, the correct way, and the only way, it does not exist.*
>
> – Friedrich Nietzsche

Deference is a poor substitute for collaboration.

Collaboration extends the power of knowing to all involved.

The person who knows it all lives in a world of ironclad

conviction: a bubble impervious to other people's ideas and beliefs. When we adhere to an unalterable perspective, we lose the potential for learning.

When I am immovable in my ideas, I must have both the first word and the final say. I must appear to have an answer for everything. This is like putting bricks in front of a doorway. No one can get in, and I cannot get out. I may feel secure behind that wall of bricks, but I will not have peace or connection.

The doorway to understanding opens with our willingness to not know; to question; to be willing to hear something diametrically opposed to our beliefs, with a true curiosity.

PeaceQ invites not-knowing into every dialogue. It initiates and welcomes the quest to learn from others.

May I be open to what I don't know
May I be willing to let my ignorance show
May I be interested in what you might teach me
and desire for new perspectives to always reach me

Gossip Can Be Good

If you want to spread some contagious happiness, talk about other people's strengths, accomplishments, and great ideas; go right ahead. When we speak about people, in their absence, with admiration and affection, we uplift the conversation and the energy in the room.

Unfortunately, this isn't how gossip usually transpires.

We live and work in close proximity to others most of the time. It is completely natural to want to talk about other people. Some of us can hear our metaphorical ears ringing when someone is speaking about us.

One of the easiest ways to start a problem, however, is to talk smack behind someone's back. When we participate in a culture of negativity, indirectness, gossip, and rumor spreading, we perpetuate emotional war.

Isn't it kind of silly to think that tearing someone else down builds you up?
– S. Sean Covey

Strong minds discuss ideas; average minds discuss events; weak minds discuss people.
– Socrates

People mistakenly think that knowing things about other people, gossiping about dirt they know, or spreading rumors gives them social capital. In truth, these actions bring only a sense of false superiority: the illusion that if I know something about you that I can share with others, I am not as puny or insignificant as I feel.

Many times, gossip springs from an issue between individuals. One feels maligned or offended by another. The first person complains to a third person about the offense. This gets the gossip mill going, and more complaint and spreading of the story—complete with the standard amount of exaggeration, conflation, and one-sidedness that characterizes the passing-along of rumors—the problem grows and becomes less manageable.

Living PeaceQ means talking directly to the person you need to talk to in order to get through a conflict. PeaceQ requires that we address people with candor and respect when we have a complaint, disagreement, resentment, or hurt. This requires courage and a willingness to be vulnerable. We may need someone else to help witness or help us prepare for a conversation, which could become intimidating or heated.

People who have full and robust social lives with deep connections and a sense of purpose do not tend to talk about others in a negative way. They spend their time promoting the best in others and highlighting their strengths.

When we refrain from talking about others disparagingly, we encourage others by example to do the same. We inherently build our self-respect and naturally steer conversation toward productive, creative, challenging topics.

The direct route to a peaceful heart is to hold others in the highest regard and seek to handle any tensions face-to-face. If we choose to take distance from someone instead of talking to them, then we should also choose being silent about them, and/or only speaking of them kindly.

Think of the air as completely pure, and think of words as either enhancing or polluting. The words we put into the air about others either opens up the skies or contaminates the air we all breathe. PeaceQ beckons us to always steer toward clean, open skies.

May I have the courage to be direct
and share myself honestly
May I speak of others for their good
and talk only as I wish others would

Exercise:

Whenever anyone starts to bag on someone else, say: "I am not so cool with talking negatively about someone. Can we move on to something awesome to talk about?"

Or: "Hey, let's talk about good things…it feels so much better."

Another route: just divert the conversation by saying, "Have you heard about…" and follow it up with something positive you are into.

105

Or, even better, you can say:

"You know something I like about you…" and then tell the person who is bagging on someone something you like about them!

For example: "The other day you made me laugh so hard when you snuck into that meeting with a big grin on your face."

How charming and disarming would that be?

How much would it positively change the tenor of the room? Of the relationship?

There is no point in shaming the person inviting you into negative gossip. They clearly need some loving too—or they would not be dragging the conversation into negative territory.

Treasuring Conflict

Peace is not absence of conflict. It is the ability to handle conflict by peaceful means.

– Ronald Reagan

Our tendency is to view conflict as bad—something to avoid or stamp out. But the "striking together" (which is what the word conflict means: from the Latin word confligiere, with con—meaning "against" and fligiere, meaning "to strike") of two pieces of wood can make an illuminating fire.

Without friction and tension, we have no growth. It is the rubbing together of our differences that makes new possibilities.

Once we realize that any truly creative venture amongst people is produced through the healthy conflict of ideas and the encouragement of feisty discussions, we can embrace conflict as an ally.

We all have different ways of dealing with conflict. Some move toward it, others move away from it, and others internalize it. Those who are especially averse to conflict may tend to give in to avoid it. Giving in doesn't resolve conflict; it buries it.

Mary doesn't want to struggle anymore with Steve over where they will send their child to school. She finally gives in and says, "Wherever you want her to go." Steve feels satisfied; Mary feels beaten down. Mary feels less engaged in decision-making and starts to withdraw. Avoiding conflict just moves the conflict down the road, piled deeper and higher.

Lauren doesn't want to upset her boss with a schedule change she wants, so she waits till the day before she needs the change to contact her boss. Lauren is now terrified and sheepish. Her boss   is upset and feels disrespected. The boss doesn't sense that Lauren is committed to the job. Lauren feels misunderstood and unfairly assessed.

Bruce wants to amend the rules of the organization and Christine disagrees. Bruce starts talking louder and more forcefully until Christine backs down. Bruce feels powerful and right; Christine feels intimidated and resentful. Engaging in conflict with loudness or aggression often leads to escalation and/or censorship.

Collaboration within a context of conflict takes understanding, patience, listening, and courage. It is the most worthwhile approach since it also leads to longer-term solutions and respect—not power over, but power with.

Blanca wants Jorge to work longer hours and take more vacation time. Jorge wants to work fewer hours and take less vacation time. They both work hard to understand the different needs from both sides. In the end, Jorge is willing to work more hours during specified times of the year, but not at other times. Both Jorge and Blanca feel understood and supportive of each other. They walk away renewed in their work relationships.

Most unresolved conflicts persist because of a lack of true communication. Show me an embedded conflict and I'll show you a situation in which people fail to meet regularly to search for common ground or practice collaborative ways to solve conflict. They may be burying the conflict, building resentment and anger in the process.

As hard as it is to move toward conflict with openness and a collaborative attitude, it is a way to lead conflict into a place where it can bear fruit for all involved. When I am heated up about a conflict, I remind myself: "We are both right! We both have valid points of view."

Once, I was angry with my colleague Jasper because I thought he had blown off an important meeting we had scheduled. When we got together to talk about the perceived slight, he explained to me that he did not feel important to the meeting because I had acted casually about his involvement. He felt irrelevant. Once we both acknowledged our parts in the misunderstanding, we were led to feel much more important to each other and our work.

> *May I see a conflict as a path to collaboration*
> *May I believe I have as much to learn as I have to say*
> *May we both have the willingness for deliberation*
> *and the courage to see it through as the better way*

Being Sorry

Remorse as an action is incredibly powerful and is often more important to intimacy than getting along. When we get along, we cruise through life amicably and sweetly, but the ruptures we encounter in every meaningful relationship are where we test our capacities to work things through and strengthen the fabric of our bonds.

If we have let someone else down, broken an agreement, or done something wrong, we feel bad. But being sorry is different from saying I am sorry. The former means taking an action that actually honors and/or repairs the trust that was broken, in a real and tangible way.

Saying "I'm sorry" does not reach past our own discomfort to comfort others. It is only a way of acknowledging that we feel bad about something.

> *Sacrifice is at the heart of repentance. Without deeds, your apology is worthless.*
>
> – Bryan Davis

When you lie to me and I find out, and you say, "I'm sorry…I'll never do it again."

…or you stay out and don't come home, and you say, "I am so sorry I didn't call."

...or you break or take something of mine and say, "God, I am so sorry."

...or you cheat on me and say, "Babe, I couldn't be more sorry—I don't know what I was thinking."

...or you forget for the 50th time to shut the drawers when I have asked you to...

...or you move me across the country to live with you and say "sorry, it's over" after a month...

...or you have had a policy of slavery for over 200 years...

...or you have created a debt crisis by irresponsible banking...

...or you have taken indigenous lands and robbed people of their livelihoods...

...saying "I'm sorry" just doesn't cut it.

Broken trust never only affects the parties directly involved in the infraction. When someone has torn the fabric of agreement, an unavoidable ripple effect occurs. Those responsible for harm live in conscious or unconscious shame, which influences their subsequent behavior. Those who have been harmed develop a tainted view of others based on being harmed, and consciously or unconsciously develop a layer of defensiveness and suspicion. They think, "If you could do that to me, who else is about to hurt or betray me?"

Accountability is not a passive state.

Accountability is *remorse* with *reparative actions*.

If we are to mend old hurts—whether personal, social, or historical—we need to find ways to actually demonstrate our remorse in compassionate and meaningful ways rather than trying to bury it, deny it, or numb ourselves against it. This is the way through resentment and entrenched distrust.

Let's say I have broken my agreement to pick you up on time for the third time. You have had to wait and worry, and it has delayed you in getting to your next appointment— which causes you to lose some credibility as well. Saying, "I'm sorry, I won't be late next time!" has little or no meaning at this point.

When we are not believable in our word, our word becomes so diluted that it occurs as a wish or hope, not a statement of fact.

On the other hand, if I say, "I have been late three times and caused you undue hardship and impact. I want to do something to repair this and make it up to you. What can I do?"—you can really think about it. You can take time to think of something that would create the possibility of my restoring my integrity.

You might say, "I would like you to do my laundry tonight, and fold everything, and do it cheerfully. This would actually make me feel like you value my time, and like you value me."

Of course, I would need to agree to your request, and the request would need to be reasonable. If all that is in place, there is a true repair. While you are doing the laundry, you also have a tangible experience of giving back my time. You can actually feel some closure instead of a perpetual sense of letting me down. Finally, of course, you will need to pick me up on time next time to avoid this cycle all over again.

Another example: You have been lying to me for years about secretive activities I had no way of knowing about because I trusted you. I only find out because someone else turns you in. Typical response: "I didn't tell you because I didn't want to hurt you. It was never about you. I am so sorry... it's over now, I'll stop." This, of course, does nothing for the person harmed by the lying. It is a flimsy bandage over the throbbing wound.

If you were to say instead, "I have totally screwed up, and this behavior is completely disrespectful to our agreement of honesty. I have no idea how to repair this because it seems so big. I cannot even fathom how you could forgive this. I would like to know if there are any ways I can repair this over time and earn back your trust? Take your time to really think about it. This will not be easy, and I will not in any way expect you to get over this fast. I am willing to do what it takes"—now, we have a beginning of restoring integrity.

There is a road back...and starting down it requires true accountability and a fervent desire to give back what has been taken in terms of trust, respect, time, and other precious things.

May I be truly sorry for the ways I have harmed
And ask, "How can I make it right?"
May I have the courage to face your pain
Making amends you suggest and bring to light

Owning Our Mistakes

Man must evolve for all human conflict a method
which rejects revenge, aggression and retaliation.
The foundation of such a method is love.
– Martin Luther King, Jr.

An admission of wrongdoing is necessary for repair. Consider, for a moment, our notions about what it means to be wrong—notions that make this admission feel, sometimes, like the proverbial Walk of Shame. If we are wrong, that means that we are our errors, false judgments, or wrong choices.

But the truth is that it isn't we who are wrong. Our core, the essence of who we are, isn't what is wrong. We are not our misjudgments, our mistakes, or our misinformation. We may have wrong thinking, mistaken facts, or even emotional distortions; however, we ourselves, in our humanness and our wholeness, are not that wrongness.

Once we realize that our perceptions, opinions, and emotions actually pass through us and are not fixed aspects of our identities, we can release our defensiveness about our stances. I have my opinions and my feelings, but they do not own me, and they do not comprise me.

For example: I might start out believing that same- sex

couples should not be allowed to marry, and I might change my mind and support marriage equality. I can do this because I am not my past or present conviction. I don't disappear when I change my mind, even if it's about something really important. I may house certain convictions, but I am fluid.

Willingness to evolve our thoughts and feelings instead of defend them like a two-year-old would cling to a play truck—"Mine! Mine! Mine!"—shows great humility and authenticity. When we learn to share ideas instead of forcing them on others and ourselves, we can entertain complexity, subtlety, and new input. We can dance through conversation instead of building armor against divergent realities.

Just as our bodies change shape over time, and just as we need to manage their changes and ultimate demise, we need to grow and change with incoming points of view and knowledge. Our precious ideas will be leaving this lifetime with us. There is no human thought form or emotion that will last in its current manifestation, so why in the world would we push against others to believe what we believe as if it meant life or death? In light of this humble perspective, it becomes easier to admit, "I have been wrong about this":

"I have been wrong about the name of that restaurant."

"I have been wrong by yelling at you for such a small thing."

"I have been wrong in doubting your decision to marry him."

115

"I have been wrong about tattoos being only for trashy people."

"I have been wrong by interrupting you so often."

"I have been wrong to create years of policies that are unequal for women."

Think of a time when someone else earnestly admitted that a belief, action, or ideal they held was wrong. How did it feel to you? Did it help you feel close to them? Did they feel closer to you? That person was building PeaceQ for both of you.

May I be eager to admit when I've been wrong
realizing that I can learn from any mistake
May I be imperfect and lovable all along
recognizing the humility that takes

Repair, Not Punishment

For me, forgiveness and compassion are always linked: how do we hold people accountable for wrongdoing and yet at the same time remain in touch with their humanity enough to believe in their capacity to be transformed.

– Bell Hooks

We take our wounds quite personally. When someone close has harmed us, it burns, torments, and tears us up. As we respond to the words and deeds of other people, we count on honesty and the other person's desire to treat us well to feel safe. We think that if only others could be infallible, we would feel a sense of impenetrable security on this out-of-control journey called life.

The truth is that any life of intimate connection and vitality will inevitably be one of euphoric hope, brutal betrayals, inconceivable disappointments, and unexpected joy.

Our instincts and emotions often run hot and cold unconsciously, or in reactivity; and sometimes, our thinking is cold and dispassionate. We have deep needs for security that often run counter to our obsessive desires for novelty and instant gratification. Our hormones rage and dim. We are not made to be consistent. We are made to adapt and evolve.

117

We all contain multitudes.

– Walt Whitman

It is a mistake to think something is wrong with life when we encounter someone or something that behaves differently from what we expect. If we truly pay attention, we notice that no one is really predictable, even as we try to box others in with our objectifying-for-security-purposes programming. When someone we care for ruins our pretty pictures of how he or she should be by behaving terribly, we have two choices:

1. Believe that the other person did this to us, which means we need to see that person as an emotional enemy. We rehearse our wounding and mull over their intentional violation of us.

2. Believe that the other person is in pain and has acted out because there is something deeper going on that might have nothing to do with us. Either way, that person's terrible behavior is ultimately his or her misfortune.

A better approach is to dislike the deed and love the person. When we separate the deed(s) and call those acts out as unacceptable, we also can have clarity about the rest of the human being. That person is not his or her best actions—or his or her worst. We may need to take space or even separate from the person whose actions have harmed us, but we will not need to carry hate in our hearts. Hating those I have loved is like amputating a part of my own body in hopes that the other parts will be stronger without the injured limb.

When we commit to loving someone who has harmed us, at whatever distance we may need to take to see his or her lovable humanity, we strengthen all parts of ourselves. We integrate the universal human shadow – the human potential to be awful—into our own development as a complete being.

Forgiveness:

...comes easiest with empathy.

...comes easiest when we do not have to continue in a harmful situation.

...is not about accepting unacceptable behaviors, but about accepting the fact that people are flawed, and that their pain will spill over onto others.

If we are truly honest, we will notice that throughout life, in small and sometimes big ways, we, too, have impacted others with our flaws and our pain.

Forgiveness also requires us to forgive ourselves for our innocence in trusting, believing, or depending on someone or something we thought would be reliable and caring. There is nothing wrong with the optimism we display in making this choice. It is far better to live with a positive frame for relationships and community than to live in skepticism and cynicism. Forgiveness actually benefits the forgiver as much, if not more, than the forgiven. When we are able to forgive our bodies relax, our attitude toward life brightens up, and we are in the possible present instead of the repeating past.

Learning to practice forgiveness for the person, even as we call out the unacceptable behavior, rescues us from living in fear of being wounded or wounding.

Living in fear truncates our ability to live an expressed life of creative possibility and unlimited connection. A fear-based approach to life actually encloses us in a smaller and smaller sphere of feeling and mobility. Sometimes it takes all our emotional strength to push beyond the pain of a transgression from someone we love to open up to life again. However: If I allow someone else's harm to close me down, I have conceded to the darkness instead of fighting for the light. If I allow harm to dictate my life instead of goodness, I set myself up to scan for reoccurring sorrow and disappointment.

Forgiving people for being flawed—even damaging——allows us to travel widely and be a magnificent part of this unending, surprising life. Choosing this is not about doing wrongdoers any favors; it is about allowing myself to move on into positive possibilities. Hanging on to hate takes up valuable creative space in my imagination and dictates how I move into new, uncharted territory. Hanging on to hate is like putting black gauze over my eyes as I look at the horizon.

As I walked out the door toward the gate that would lead to my freedom, I knew if I didn't leave my bitterness and hatred behind, I'd still be in prison.
– Nelson Mandela

If, instead, you can simply love the people you have loved—
whether or not you can ever forget their damaging acts—
you move toward that brilliantly sparkling horizon line
of your own dreams and desires, seeing through a wide-
angle lens of both shadow and light.

> *May I forgive the person even as I dislike the deed*
> *understanding that we are all flawed*
> *May I see the best in people even as they stumble*
> *and believe that I too can be that humble*

Learning to Speak with Respect and to Use Honorable Language

The best of us must sometimes eat our words.

– J.K. Rowling

Words can be weapons, and words can be bridges. Words can tear people apart or bring people closer together. "Political Correctness" sometimes hinders us from speaking spontaneously when it becomes too shaming, and yet the conscious use of respectful and inclusive language really matters. The trick is to be earnest in our desire to know the power and impact of our words and be willing to learn how to uplift people with our words instead of hurting them. A good rule of thumb I use is to refrain from saying anything that anyone might find offensive if they overheard it. This practice can also save us all public humiliation in the day of inconspicuous recording devices.

Words describe our reality. From them, the stories we tell each other about our lives, our perspectives, our emotions, and our needs are constructed.

There are over 250,000 words in the English dictionary. The more words we know and use, the more descriptive we can be in communicating the full spectrum of our daily experience. The more detailed we can be in communicating our emotional lives, the more likely it is that we will be intimately known.

Most of us use less than one percent of the English language. That's like taking a sliver of your fingertip and using only that part of your body to express yourself; then wondering, "Why don't people get me?"

Over 10,000,000 shades of color can be identified by the human eye. What if we used the same five colors on every painting we ever painted? What if we put the same color line through every shape we drew? What if we limited everyone to wearing the same primary colors of clothing or driving only the same five pastel colors of cars? Surely, many would protest: "You are taking away my freedom. You are limiting my choices!"

Many of us speak like we have only a limited choice of words. Many of us use curse words as though they were our most powerful tools of communication.

Words, like colors, are free to everyone. Any of us can learn to express and bring vitality to our worlds with original combinations and revelatory narratives.

Swearing or cursing can become that one-color line, overused to emphasize every sentence or idea. A few curse words become our go-to choice for punctuation and intense expression. They often become unoriginal fillers or blotters for complex thoughts, feelings, or ideas. People who speak with a wide and descriptive vocabulary are more widely effective in communicating with others. Speech consistently laced with expletives becomes routine and repetitive and ultimately loses its significance: not renegade or thrilling, but tedious. Frequent listeners come to count on delivery of frequent curse bombs: same flavor, same amount, same packaging…every time.

The question is: Do you want to be dispensing an ordinary, routine, mindless, predictable f***ing side of the conversation?

Or do you want to deliver unique, powerful messages that mark you as someone to listen to and someone to know?

Example: (When expressing your views to someone who disagrees with you politically): That politician is such a *** ^ ^ ^ ^ that I cannot stand to hear him. He is so f********* and so d******* and so c***** I wish he would *******disappear.

Instead: That politician expresses such loud and angry disdain for immigrants that I have trouble listening to what he says. He seems so emotionally careless, and he often says disparaging things about women. I am concerned about his influence on people who are looking for role models because he does command a lot of media and attention. I wish the political conversation was more about issues and encouraged people to speak with maturity and respect.

> *May I use words as candles to illuminate all I can*
> *Opening up language like a colorful wingspan*
> *May I learn new and descriptive words every day*
> *And become someone who has something unique*
> *and wise to say*

Part Three

Peace In Our Communities

Whereas peace within creates a serene disposition, and peace with others instills a sense of connection and promotes healthy relationships, peace in our communities is about extending our practices to include and embrace others until PeaceQ surrounds the globe.

Connection Circles: Putting PeaceQ Into Practice

One of the key means of developing PeaceQ in our communities and in ourselves is facilitation of, and participation in, Connection Circles. Connection Circles can happen anywhere between two or more people and involve an engaged and voluntary interest in deep listening and honest sharing. While there are hundreds of valuable ways to work for peace, Connection Circles can be basic building blocks to create a foundation of understanding and communication that will enable the furthering of any committed endeavor for harmony.

Connection Circles require one or two facilitators committed to holding a circle in which only one person speaks at a time and where every person's voice is honored and matters.

All involved must agree that the circle is explicitly different from everyday conversation in which there is back and forth, interruption, and competition for the floor.

Connection Circles are held in an environment where others can be heard without distraction; participants agree to refrain from drinking and eating and shut off all digital devices and distractions.

Connection Circles are:

An antidote to an overly technological, attention-deficit culture.

An event unique and separate from everyday life that brings a sense of ritual and sacredness to all participants.

A way to highlight commitment to being in an altered time and space where each person takes time to pay attention to what is being shared.

Connection Circles offer relief from needing to have our voice matter more than someone else's. They give an opportunity for shy, reluctant speakers to feel heard in equal standing for perhaps the first time. In our culture of extroversion, Connection Circles are a simple, reliable way to create a true democracy of voice.

I have taught Connection Circle leadership for over twenty years. Here are some of the comments I've heard about the impact of circles in their lives:

"This is the first time I've really felt like our family has been able to listen to each other without arguing, and now I wouldn't have a Sunday dinner without it."

– 46-year-old father of three

"I finally have been able to understand people who don't look like me and talk like me. This has changed my life."

– 15-year-old high school student

"I finally could listen to somebody who does not share my religious or political beliefs and really take in their context and their point of view."

– 33-year-old woman

"These connection circles have helped me feel much closer to my colleagues and made me much more willing to work with them."

– 19 year-old employee

Connection Circles Guidelines

Connection Circles can occur between two people or as many as 30 people at one time. They are run according to six guidelines:

1. Only speak when you have the talking piece.

There is no cross-talk in the Connection Circle format. To ensure that only one person speaks at any time, Connection Circles utilize a talking piece agreed upon by the group. It can be something sacred and special (an amulet, a beautiful rock, a beloved stuffed animal) or something mundane (a pencil, a leaf, a scarf). The point of the talking piece is to ensure that only one person speaks at a time, and hands over the talking piece to the next participant only when the speaker is done speaking.

2. Speak with respect from the heart.

When it is your turn to speak, let the words flow from your heart. If there is a silence as someone holds the talking piece and gathers his or her thoughts, let that be okay. Sometimes silence is the sharing. Someone may choose simply to hold the talking piece and reflect. Not all sharing is verbal.

3. Listen with respect from the heart.

In everyday conversation we often anticipate what others will say and listen as if we know what is coming next. Listening from the heart is about being willing to not have a fixed notion of what the person will say. Listen to others with total attention. Notice judgments you may have about what others say, but don't get attached to them. Use the opportunity of sitting together in circle to see and hear the person exactly as he or she is.

4. Be concise when it is your turn to share.

Ensure that everyone has an opportunity to share within the time allowed for the circle by being concise with your own sharing. Don't leave anything important out, but make every word count, and don't let yourself go on and on.

5. Be spontaneous when you share.

Do not mentally rehearse while others are sharing. Let yourself share whatever comes up when the talking piece is in your hands and you have taken a good deep breath before starting to speak.

6. Keep the privacy of the circle.

Connection Circle participants promise to keep whatever is said in the circle in confidence; the only exception is where a participant wants to share his or her own experience outside the circle. This is fine, as long as that person does not bring in anyone else's experience.*

* *Confidentiality may need to be broken if you are a mandated reporter or have knowledge that someone may cause imminent harm to themselves or another.*

Getting Others to Sit In Connection Circles

I had one student who wanted to have a Connection Circle with her in-laws and her biological family. At first, her attitude with those family members was, "This is going to be good for you, so you'd *better*," and nobody wanted to do it.

As you try to get others to sit in Circles with you, hold a policy of "attraction not promotion." We cannot force someone else to connect with us. Connection, by its very nature, is about vulnerability, willingness, and curiosity.

When inviting people into a Circle, help them feel safe by making it about positivity, creativity, joy, and a deep, sharing spirit. "This is good for you, so DO IT!" will not promote voluntary or authentic sharing. Be open, curious, and loving. Let go of enrolling people; take a tack opposite to proselytizing.

When the student shifted her approach and said, "I would like to listen to and get to know you all better and understand your points of view," her Connection Circles were a huge success. Family members listened to each other in ways they had never listened before.

How to Lead a Connection Circle

Always keep in mind that Connection Circle leadership is characterized by curiosity and humor, not contempt or criticism. It is not judgmental or heavy-handed. As leader, always remember that everyone is doing the best they can in the moment.

1. Start off by making sure everybody has a comfortable seat. Let them know that it is perfectly OK to stretch and move and change their positions—to have comfort in their physical body in order to listen.

2. Let them know you will be facilitating and always going first.

3. Let them know that the only person who may talk at any time is the person with the talking piece.

4. Establish a signal the facilitator can use if somebody is monopolizing too much time by accident. This happens to the best of us while speaking from the heart; it is not difficult to lose track of what we're saying and forget how long we've been talking. Come up with a signal at the beginning: time-out, hand on heart, wrap it up, get to the point, tick-tock. Discuss what might be a fair amount of time for each participant to share,

given the amount of time you have for the circle and the number of participants. Make this part of the initial agreements.

5. If you do not have pre-set questions for the question rounds (which come after the check- in; see below), ask the group what questions might be a good fit for that day's circle.

6. Check-in: The Thorns and Roses (T & R) check-in gives each person in the circle a chance to share something that isn't going well (thorn) and something that is going well (rose) with the rest of the group. The facilitator shares first to give participants a clear sense of what is expected, then passes the talking stick to let the next person begin.

7. Question round: Once T&R are finished, begin the first question round (see next chapter for suggested questions and guidelines for creating your own questions).

8. Repeat with new questions. A typical circle will go through two to three questions.

9. A round of expressions of gratitude/ appreciations is a good way to finish a Connection Circle. Each person can share a single word about what he or she is grateful for or give an appreciation to someone else in the circle or about the circle experience in general.

Suitable Connection Circle Questions

Choose questions that are open-ended (not yes/ no) and elicit thoughtful sharing, not judgment or a "performance" designed to try to impress others.

Example: "Name a time you felt truly successful in something that you put a lot of effort into."

As the facilitator, I would answer first, sharing something like: "The time we held a conference for 200 student AHA! Peace Builders and watched them conduct their own Connection Circles, which they had learned to do from a previous training." Then, I would pass the talking piece and others would answer in turn.

Other examples of good Connection Circle questions are below. Some are more serious; others more lighthearted and fun. As you gain experience with Circle leadership, you will develop an instinct for choosing the right kinds of questions for whatever group you find gathered with you.

Name a time that you felt excluded. What was that like?

Name a time that you felt included. What was that like?

What can you do to be more inclusive toward others?

Who is a role model for you and why?

Tell about a person in your life who you didn't think you liked or loved, but who taught you something important.

Share about a place or time where you felt a lack of confidence.

Share about a place or a time where you felt a lot of confidence.

What interrupts our confidence? How do we regroup when we fail?

If you could have a soundtrack to your life, what would be the intro song?

If you were stranded on a desert island, what three items would you choose to have with you?

If you could have any heightened sense, what would it be?

If you could walk on water or breathe under water, which would you choose? Why?

During a natural disaster, what three items would you grab right away?

Who would you want to play you in a movie? Why?

If you were to be a leader of a nation, would you want the biggest army or the biggest educational budget? Why?

What is the cleverest thing you have ever gotten away with?

If karma were to bite you in the butt, what would it do to you?

What is the most private thing you are willing to admit?

What was your worst date, ever?

What is the silliest thing you did as a kid?

If you had to be named another name, what would you call yourself?

If you were one article of clothing, what would you be? Why?

Describe your first crush.

Describe the most beautiful thing you have ever seen.

If you were immortal for a day, what would you do?

If you had to be the other gender, who would you be? Why?

What's your superhero name?

If you had a time machine that would work only once, what point in the future or history would you visit?

If you could talk to any one person now living, who would it be and why?

If I gave you $10,000, what would you spend it on?

Leading with Peace Questions: A Meditation

Bringing a positive mood and attitude to a Connection Circle before beginning can make a big difference. Depth, openness, and vulnerability all expand in a positive space. You can create this kind of positive space through Resource Tapping, which I described on pages 56-58. I have used this method in many groups now, and have found it to be a really simple and useful way of "dropping in" that aligns well with the aims of Connection Circles and PeaceQ. Try it for a few moments with your Connection Circle and notice the lift in the group's mood.

You may also choose to set the tone of a circle through a meditation like the one described below.

As a leader, engage in this meditation often. Let it guide your Connection Circle leadership. Share it with participants; use it as a circle opening or closing.

Three deep breaths, then:

May I be at peace

May you be at peace

May we be at peace

Am I leading with an attitude of inspiration and possibility?

Am I actively demonstrating an interest in people who seem different from me?

Am I using language that invites everyone to be respected and honored?

Am I reaching out for support when I am confused, hurt, or misunderstood?

Am I acknowledging others for all the various ways they contribute and express themselves?

Am I making space and time for all kinds of voices and opinions to be heard?

Am I offering opportunities and experiences that connect people across all lines of race, economic, and gender identities?

Am I welcoming creative ideas to enhance and enliven conversation and connection?

Am I standing up for anyone who is being slighted, teased, or rejected in any way?

Three deep breaths, then:

May I learn with joy

May you learn with joy

May we learn with joy

Restorative Versus Punitive

Connection Circles are foundational building blocks, creating a community that listens deeply, displays empathy, and seeks to remain whole. The restorative approach maintains that every person who has committed harm, if willing, can repair that harm to the best of their ability and to the degree the harmed are willing to receive that repair.

The punishment model involves the disciplining and correcting of the offender(s) by an authoritative body. It customarily results in separation, humiliation, and loss of dignity and/or freedom for the offenders. Punitive discipline also fails to facilitate emotional closure for the harmed, who are kept from the powerful catharsis possible with letting their offenders know how they feel and what they need to become whole again.

The punishment model of discipline has persevered throughout time thanks to the idea that harming the harmer through harsh punishment or sequestration will end the harm. We now know that removing an offender from his or her community rarely rehabilitates that person, and that corporal punishment has not reformed offenders. Most young people who are separated and shamed by the punishment model develop a pattern of further harm or self-harm.

We now know that incarceration rarely rehabilitates anyone, and that violence has not been extinguished by violence. What many of us do not know is that the prison system has become a for-profit business in the United States. Private prison companies actually work to get 100% occupancy rates.

On the other hand, the restorative approach to justice and discipline has borne great fruit. Communities who actively practice this repair model—which involves restitution and remorse, and is fulfilled upon detailed contracts of repair—are actually seeing extraordinary drops in recidivism.

In one 2005 meta-analysis of studies conducted over 25 years in New Zealand, only 20 percent of offenders who participated in a restorative justice (RJ) program went on to reoffend, while 48 percent of those who did not participate in RJ programs did commit another crime. In other words, a restorative approach to justice more than halved the recidivism rate. The restorative model involves all parties harmed having both a face-to-face dialogue with the person who has committed the harm and an actual say in what would be a meaningful repair for them. The result: The harmed actually can move through the intense and unbearable feelings of victimization and/or pain, and the harming party or parties actually learn to see the impact of their actions.

Restorative processes maintain that all people who have committed harm can repair that harm, as long as they themselves are willing and as long as those harmed are willing to receive that repair. If someone who has committed harm is not willing to take full responsibility and address his or her impact on others, that offender will choose the loneliness and exile of the punishment model.

> *Instead of suspending kids from school or in addition to suspending kids from school, what about actually getting everybody to talk about what happened?... For a young person to have to...face the people he or she has harmed and... learn how he or she has impacted them can be very effective. Punishment is very passive; you get punished and you don't have any responsibility. You get to be angry at the people who suspended you. But really, you don't get the opportunity to think about how you affected other people.*

– Ted Wachtel,
President and Founder of the
International Institute for Restorative Practices (IIRP)

Restorative processes allow all parties harmed to have:

1. A face-to-face dialogue with the person who has committed the harm; and

2. An actual say in what would be a meaningful repair for them.

As a result, the harmed can move through the intense and unbearable feelings of victimization and/or pain. The harming party or parties learn to see the impact of their actions and to have a tangible road back to integrity.

*I am continually humbled by human capacities
for openness, heart-centered connecting,
humility, compassion, understanding, and love.
I find that restorative justice in general and
peacemaking circles in particular help us connect
with our deepest and best selves and bring these
dimensions of ourselves to some of the hardest
challenges we face.*

– Kay Pranis, author and nationally known
Restorative Justice advocate

Connection Circles create opportunities for communities to listen deeply, express empathy, and seek to remain intact. In schools and communities that practice the art of Connection Circles, a harm done to one person is actually recognized as a break in the wholeness of community life. When there is a break in the community due to wrongdoing on the part of one or more community members, Connection Circles can be a safe space for restorative processes.

When someone causes harm, our traditional system asks:

1. What rule was broken?

2. Who broke it?

3. What punishment is deserved?

To enact a restorative process within a Connection Circle, all parties harmed can sit with those who have done harm to ask and answer these questions:

1. What harm was done and to whom?

2. Who has been impacted? What needs have arisen in those people, based on this harm?

3. Who is responsible to repair the harm, and how can that repair be made and accounted for in a timely and measurable way?

A restorative process could be implemented following review of guidelines, check-in, and one or two question rounds to bring all participants into the same positive, empathic field—the best place from which to enact restoration.

People who actively practice this repair model are seeing extraordinary drops in repeat offenses and saving school districts significant money. Suspension and expulsion rates are being drastically reduced. Young people are becoming more productive and proud.

Sitting in circle to restore integrity is a visceral demonstration to the harming parties that they are not alone. In the circle, they experience their transgressions as not only having caused harm to others, but also as offering the potential for life- changing lessons, redemption, and reinstatement as valued members of the community.

May I long to keep the circle unbroken
if there is a chance for integrity and repair
May I work to restore inevitable ruptures
and build communities that are whole, just, and fair

Connection Circles and Restorative Approaches are modes by which all of us can participate in a devoted practice of PeaceQ in our communities. Whether you are at home with family, or in an institutional or company setting, these tools and ideas can be implemented with willing participants and promote an atmosphere of harmony and understanding. We cannot change our sense of oppression or injustice with hostile dialogue or takeovers. We have seen that one deafening dominant paradigm replacing another is just more of the same in a different guise. When we all take the time to listen and learn from one another the possibility for genuine sharing is more likely. We will also be more creative and more likely to reflect the best of our diverse perspectives.

One summer, years ago, AHA! was holding its summer session for high school students at a local private middle school. A week into the session, two AHA! teens "Juan" and "Larry" broke into the school after the summer session hours, destroyed some desks, and defaced property with tagging. They were caught.

Instead of summarily kicking these boys out of the program, we took the day to have a restorative process with them. While sitting in circle, the other teens and adult facilitators spoke to Juan and Larry about the impact of their actions as well as about their value to the program. Larry and Juan took full responsibility for the harm they committed and worked with the group and the school officials to determine how they could repair for their actions. They agreed to clean up the school for a period of time and work to pay off the property damage. The boys responded thoughtfully to how their behavior jeopardized the AHA! program and the reputation of the other teens. There was a lot of crying and genuine remorse from the two boys. The group also got to know Juan and Larry better and heard about how that particular school had been the site of intense bullying for Larry when he was a student there. Larry admitted that he was taking out his hatred for his past bullying experience on the school.

Juan and Larry were reintegrated back into the group for that summer session. They completed all their agreements with the school and became closer to the rest of the teens. The other teens said that this was the first time in their lives they saw something bad turn into something good.

Both young men went on to do well in their lives and have stayed in contact with AHA! with pride and gratitude.

Onward

Congratulations you have read this book and have begun the journey to:

1. Learning how to be more peaceful inside ourselves.

2. Learning how to create satisfying and harmonious relationships with others.

3. Learning how to actively cultivate loving and peaceful connections in our communities.

The practice of PeaceQ is just that, a practice. There is no "getting it." I am learning every day how to bring more peace into my life. Some days it is two steps backwards... and then another three steps falling down before I get up and am able to utilize the principles with grace. I have learned to laugh much quicker at myself when I screw up, which makes it much easier to admit and share my imperfections with others.

What is important is that every day we practice and inspire others to practice too. PeaceQ can be practiced alone, and the book can be a bedside companion to remind us of our truest and most loving selves. When we are able to practice PeaceQ with others, our abilities and efforts magnify. In a community of dedicated learners we increase the vibration and attention to PeaceQ. That is why we have developed the website www. peaceq.com so we can hear your stories of

PeaceQ in action, keep track of your efforts, and to answer your questions as you face obstacles or slumps in your practice. Imagine PeaceQ being practiced by millions on a daily basis. Imagine the ripples we can make.

IT BEGINS WITH YOU!

**If you are interested in our PeaceQ ambassador training please contact me directly at www.jenniferfreed.com

[APPENDIX]
The PeaceQ Online Application

The PeaceQ website application is a way for you to keep track of your progress in building your own PeaceQ, and to document the impact you make on your community through Connection Circles.

Whether you are involved in a school, a religious organization, a spiritual group, a professional office or organization, an agency, or you are an individual wanting to improve your PeaceQ, the website application at www.peaceq.com can help you: Keep track of your Peace Points—the ways you are actively bringing peace to your community in your daily life.

1. Record the outstanding behavior of others, which helps you look for the best in others as well as reinforcing your own brain's positive neurological connections.

2. Keep actual data on your self-care, helping you to see objectively how well you are doing at caring for your body, mind, feelings, and spirit and affirming every step you take to becoming more whole and healthy.

3. Document your Connection Circles with others,

helping you realize how much inspiring influence you can have each time you facilitate a sacred sharing from the heart/deep listening.

The website application was designed to be easy, accessible, and entirely focused on positive brain psychology because we know now what we focus our attention on dictates how we feel. Why not subscribe to this website application and become part of a world effort to bring peace within, peace with others, and peace to our communities?

AHA! students have been using the website application (www.peaceq.com) to record their Connection Circles.

The PeaceQ app has been a great tool for gathering data on this program when it's used with youth. But it has value beyond this.

When we do a thing, and we record it; and then when someone else sees us doing it, and then reflects back to us that we are successfully doing it…that's very reinforcing. Positive regard is built much more quickly under these circumstances than if we are flying solo, just trying to do or be good without keeping track or having our good doings reflected back to us.

Being held in that light helps us feel a building benefit in holding Connection Circles, enhancing our own PeaceQ and being an envoy of PeaceQ toward others.

People say walking on water is a miracle, but to me walking peacefully on earth is the real miracle.

– Thich Nhat Hanh

Resources

Please refer to the books and websites listed below to find out more about Restorative Justice, which is also referred to as Restorative Approaches.

The Way of Council by Jack Zimmerman and Virginia Coyle (1996)

Building and Restoring Respectful Relationships in Schools: A Guide to Restorative Practice by Richard Hendry (2009)

Just Schools: A Whole School Approach to Restorative Justice by Belinda Hopkins (2003)

Mediation and Restoration in Circle Time by Teresa Bliss (1999)

Restorative Solutions: Making It Work by Colin Newton and Helen Mahaffey (2008)

Books and Other Resources for Further Inspiration
Some of these books were direct resources for this one; others are offered as inspirations to you along your PeaceQ journey.

Nonfiction Books
A Long Way Gone: Memoirs of a Boy Soldier by Ishmael Beah (2007)

A Thousand Names for Joy: Living in Harmony With the Way Things Are by Byron Katie and Stephen Mitchell (2007)

Before Happiness by Shawn Achor (2013)

Bird by Bird: Some Instructions on Writing and Life by Anne Lamott (1995)

Brainstorm by Daniel Siegel (2013)

Check Your Attitude at the Door: The Power of Positive Intention by James Peal (2012)

Help, Thanks, Wow: The Three Essential Prayers by Anne Lamott (2012)

Daring Greatly: How the Courage to Be Vulnerable Transforms the Way We Live, Love, Parent, and Lead by Brené Brown (2012)

How to Love by Thich Nhat Hanh and Jason DeAntonis (2014)

Loving What Is: Four Questions That Can Change Your Life by Byron Katie and Stephen Mitchell (2002)

Outrageous Openness by Tosha Silver (2014)

Small Victories: Spotting Improbable Moments of Grace by Anne Lamott (2014)

Start Where You Are: A Guide to Compassionate Living by Pema Chodron (2010)

Teaching Peace by Beverly Brown Title (2011)

The Art of Communicating by Thich Nhat Hanh (2013)

The Four Agreements: A Practical Guide to Personal Freedom by Don Miguel Ruiz (1997)

The Happiness Advantage by Sean Achor (2010)

Triumph of the Heart: Forgiveness in an Unforgiving World by Megan Feldman Bettencourt (2015)

When Things Fall Apart: Heart Advice for Difficult Times by Pema Chodron (2010)

Writing Down the Bones by Natalie Goldberg (2nd Edition, 2005)

Web Sites to Explore
www.selpractices.org

www.casel.org

www.6seconds.org

www.byronkatie.com

www.brenebrown.com

www.pemachodronfoundation.org

http://ojaifoundation.org

Novels to Open Your Heart

Reading novels and memoirs is essential for building PeaceQ. Stories are the best way to learn about other people and other cultures. A great novel touches a place in all of us that can relate.

A Lesson Before Dying by Ernest Gaines (2004)

All The Light We Cannot See by Anthony Doerr (2014)

Americanah by Chimamanda Ngozi Adichie (2014)

Ceremony by Leslie Marmon Silko (2006)

Kindred by Octavia Butler (2004)

Like Water for Chocolate: A Novel in Monthly Installments with Recipes, Romances, and Home Remedies by Laura Esquivel (2002)

Middlesex by Jeffrey Eugenides (2002)

Night by Elie Wiesel (2012)

Oranges are Not the Only Fruit by Jeanette Winterson (2007)

Princess: A True Story of Life Behind the Veil in Saudi Arabia by Jean Sasson (2014)

Push by Sapphire (1997)

Rain of Gold by Victor E. Villaseñor (2015)

Shanghai Girls by Lisa See (2009)

Shark Dialogues by Kiana Davenport (2010)

Song of Solomon by Toni Morrison (2007)

Stones from the River by Ursula Hegi (2011)

The Book of Ruth by Jane Hamilton (2014)

The Chronicles of Narnia by C.S. Lewis (multiple ed.)

The Color Purple by Alice Walker (2003)

The Invention of Wings by Sue Monk Kidd (2014)

The Reader by Bernhard Schlink (2001)

The Rosie Project: A Novel by Graeme Simsion (2013)

Unbroken: A World War II Story of Survival, Resilience, and Redemption by Laura Hillenbrand (2010)

Wild: From Lost to Found on the Pacific Crest Trail by Cheryl Strayed (2012)

Zeitoun by Dave Eggers (2010)

Specific Resources on Parenting and Education

Building and Restoring Respectful Relationships in Schools: A Guide to Restorative Practice by Richard Hendry (2009)

Just Schools: A Whole School Approach to Restorative Justice by Belinda Hopkins (2003)

Mediation and Restoration in Circle Time by Teresa Bliss (1999)

Restorative Solutions: Making It Work by Colin Newton and Helen Mahaffey (2008)

Parenting/Education/Web Sites to Explore

www.drrobertbrooks.com

www.rontaffel.com

http://rjoyoakland.org/restorative-justice/

Other Titles by Jennifer Freed, PhD

Lessons from Stanley the Cat: Nine Lives of Everyday Wisdom (2010)

The Become Your Best Self workbook series (2007, edited by Amanda Waldman Lake)
> *Character: Empowering Yourself With Emotional Intelligence*
> *Compassion: Diversity Education and Prejudice Reduction*
> *Relationship Wisdom: Healthy Sexuality and Self Respect*
> *Creative Expression: Creativity and Self Exploration*

The Ultimate Personality Guide: Forget the Shrinks, Forget the Psychics, Analyze Yourself! (2001, with Debra Birnbaum)

Acknowledgments

*If we have no peace, it is because we have
forgotten that we belong to each other.*

– Mother Teresa

This list could literally be as long as this book. The best of
me is truly an amalgam of every phenomenal person I have
been lucky enough to know. If you have walked beside
me at some point on this path and find yourself not listed
here, it is only due to my less than sterling memory; it
does not reflect on your worth and importance in my life.

I want to thank my earliest influences on my quest for
PeaceQ:

…My parents Nancy and Bert Freed, and my Aunt Jane,
who instilled in me from day one a passion for social
justice and an enduring love of life

…my dearest brother Carl: You showed me patience and
kindness, even when I tested you mercilessly;

…my first real love, Wendell, who gave me a sense of
harmony and peace I had never known;

…Jaclyn, who taught me how to be vulnerable instead of
defensive;

...and Lynne and Cathy, my patient guides through legions of pain.

I also want to thank my teachers, who have dedicated their lives to an equitable and peaceful world: Brent Blair, Augusto Boal, Brené Brown, Jennifer Buffett, Peter Buffett, Howie Cohn, Gigi Coyle and Jack Zimmerman, Susan Crown, Anne Davin, Angela Hudson and Katy Perry, Byron Katie, Laurel Parnell, Jim Peal, Tosha Silver, Richard Tarnas, Beverly Title, Mary Watkins, and my cat Stanley (he has his own book).

I want to thank my editors: Melissa Lowenstein, who could truly write the world anew and we would all be grateful; and Tiana Leeds, who jumped in to help. Tom Sturgess became my knight in shining honor when I needed guidance the most.

Georgia Freedman donated her expertise in the most important and generous ways.

Lisa Foley and Carol Kline gave precious insights.

I want to thank Molly Green for countless consultations and whose light refracts the best of all of us.

I want to thank the Board of AHA!, the "Devo" angels, and the staff of AHA!, and District Superintendent Dave Cash, who give themselves entirely to the notion that PeaceQ is not a dream, but a coming-soon reality. I am indebted to the thousands of AHA! teens who practice PeaceQ and teach me about love every day.

I want to thank the mermaids who make me remember why it all matters and help me laugh harder than I cry.

Beautiful Josh Wand designed the PeaceQ application and has been exceptionally patient with all the revisions and the technical demands.

Finally, I want to thank my best two teachers: Jan Scott Fadden, who has committed her entire life to loving kindness; and Rendy Freedman, who has taught me what peace in everyday practice looks like, and who is the reason I believe in love everlasting.

About the Author

Jennifer Freed Ph.D. is the Executive Director of AHA! www.ahasb.org and lives in Santa Barbara, California. Please learn more about her at www.jenniferfreed.com.